A Guided Tour of
John Stuart Mill's
Utilitarianism

A Guided Tour of John Stuart Mill's *Utilitarianism*

Julius Jackson
San Bernardino Valley College

Series Editor
Christopher Biffle

Mayfield Publishing Company
Mountain View, California
London • Toronto

Copyright © 1993 by Mayfield Publishing Company

Library of Congress Cataloging-in-Publication Data

Jackson, Julius
    A guided tour of John Stuart Mill's Utilitarianism / Julius Jackson.
        p.   cm.
    Includes bibliographical references.
    ISBN 1-55934-096-7 (paper)
    1. Mill, John Stuart, 1806–1873.   Utilitarianism
  2. Utilitarianism. I. Title.
  B1603.U873J33   1992
  171′.5—dc20   92-25431
                                          CIP

Manufactured in the United States of America

10 9 8 7 6 5 4 3 2

Mayfield Publishing Company
1240 Villa Street
Mountain View, California 94041

Sponsoring editor, James Bull; production editor, Carol Zafiropoulos. This text was set in 10/12 Palatino by ExecuStaff and printed on 50# Finch Opaque by Malloy Lithographing.

Excerpts from *Kant: Foundations of the Metaphysics of Morals,* translated by Lewis White Beck, reprinted with the permission of Macmillan Publishing Company, Inc. Copyright © 1959 by Macmillan Publishing Company.

Extracts from *The Philosophy of Epicurus* by George K. Strodach reprinted with the permission of Northwestern University Press.

"Letter from Birmingham Jail" from *Why We Can't Wait* by Martin Luther King, Jr. Copyright © 1963, 1964 by Martin Luther King, Jr. Reprinted by permission of Harper-Collins Publishers.

Extracts from *An Introduction to the Principles of Morals and Legislation,* edited by J. H. Burns and H. L. A. Hart. Copyright © University of London, 1970. Reprinted with the permission of the Athlone Press.

Contents

Preface

To the Instructor

This book will help your students get the most out of reading John Stuart Mill's *Utilitarianism*. Designed for the novice in philosophy, it contains the complete text of *Utilitarianism*, supplemented by tasks that help students develop their philosophical thinking, reading, and writing skills.

My philosophy students need a lot of practice in orderly thinking and writing. They need practice in following a logical pattern, giving reasons for assertions, clarifying points with examples, and quoting supporting material from a text. Plenty of opportunities for such practice are provided here.

In general, the annotation tasks in the margins are appropriate for a first reading: Students underline key sentences, paraphrase main ideas, and construct relevant examples. The fill-in-the-blank dialogues between myself and the reader guide students through rereading and rethinking central passages. These sections may be used as homework assignments (photocopy and hand in), as in-class writing assignments, or as the focus of small group work.

To make your students' first encounter with *Utilitarianism* even more fruitful, I have included the following:

- A brief introduction to Mill's life and thought,
- Summaries of each chapter of *Utilitarianism*,
- Substantial related reading selections, with annotations, by Epicurus, Jeremy Bentham, Immanuel Kant, and Martin Luther King, Jr.,

- A brief appendix, Writing about Ethics and John Stuart Mill,
- A list of suggested further readings.

If this work contributes to the conversation of philosophy, I would like to acknowledge those who have contributed to my ability to converse: my teachers, especially Ron Massanari, David Miller, and Pat Cox Miller; my colleagues, especially Bill Johnson, Bill Schweiker, and Chris Biffle; my wife, Jan Ropp Jackson; and my students—especially all those courageous students over the years who were willing to look me in the eye and say, with complete honesty and sincerity, "I don't understand." They have enabled the conversation that is philosophy to continue even when I have tried to close it off.

I would also like to thank the following pre-publication reviewers for their excellent suggestions and advice: Frank Fair, Sam Houston State University; William Lawhead, University of Mississippi; Donald Palmer, College of Marin; and Becky Cox White, California State University, Chico.

To the Student

My primary goal in this book is to guide you through a very important work in the history of philosophy, John Stuart Mill's *Utilitarianism*. I have found that students benefit from a variety of different pedagogical approaches, and I have combined many of them here. Not everything in this book will help you understand the material, but the odds are good that this tour will help you read *Utilitarianism* more slowly, carefully, and responsively than you otherwise would, and this, I believe, will be time well spent.

A Guided Tour of
John Stuart Mill's
Utilitarianism

PART 1
Introduction

An Introduction to John Stuart Mill's *Utilitarianism*

Before you begin your guided tour of John Stuart Mill's classic work, *Utilitarianism,* there are a few things you should know. First of all, this introduction will tell you something about the fundamental question that Mill addresses in this text. Then it will describe Mill's life and the cultural setting for his writing and thinking and place Mill's work within the broader history of philosophy. Next it will briefly summarize the chapters of *Utilitarianism.* Finally the introduction will help you practice reading difficult philosophical texts. Mill's writing style is a very dense, complicated, nineteenth-century British prose. Reading Mill is not like reading *Time* magazine or a newspaper. So the last task of the introduction is to give you some practical suggestions about actually reading this important piece of philosophy.

With the introduction behind you, reading Mill's words and thinking through his ideas will be much more rewarding.

The Question of Ethics

One definition of philosophy is "thinking critically about questions that matter."[1] With this definition, philosophy is based on a set of questions such as: What is beauty?; What is the good life?; What is reality?; How does one know what is real? While these are important, another question that matters is: What should I (or we) do? Another way to ask this is: How does one determine right action?

---

[1] Ed. L. Miller, *Questions That Matter* (New York: McGraw-Hill, 1987), p. 14.

Reflection on this question creates the philosophical field called ethics. Imagine that you and your best friend are taking an exam in the same class. You glance up and witness your best friend blatantly cheating on the exam. What should you do? What is the right thing to do? Should you do anything at all? As you reflect on this scenario you are involved in the process of determining right or good action; you are reflecting on the philosophical discipline called ethics. If you have ever questioned whether it is right for American companies to do business in South Africa where they support the oppressive system of apartheid, you have reflected on what you (or we) should do. Ethics is concerned with how we make those judgments of proper behavior. Ethics asks: On what basis or according to what set of characteristics can we determine right from wrong?

Mill's *Utilitarianism* is a work that is based on the question of right action. *Utilitarianism* asks: How do we know what we should do? This is an ancient question in philosophy, but Mill's genius in *Utilitarianism* is that he appeals to a classic criterion of right behavior (i.e., happiness) but places it in a new, socially oriented context. A popular version of the principle of utilitarianism is ''act so that your actions will create the greatest amount of happiness for the greatest number of people.'' This becomes Mill's answer to the question of ethics: What is the right thing to do in any situation? Mill's response is that the right thing to do creates the most happiness for the greatest number of people. While there are some problems with this line of thinking, it continues to be an influential ethical tradition in today's world.

Mill's Life

Mill was born in London in 1806, C.E.[2] His father was the famous economist and social philosopher, James Mill. James Mill was determined that his son would carry out and spread the philosophy that he and his colleague Jeremy Bentham had developed. They called this philosophy ''utilitarianism.'' To ensure the proper development of young John, James Mill supervised his son's education. And it was a remarkable education. Mill studied Greek at age three and Latin at age eight. By the age of fourteen, Mill had been thoroughly schooled in the classics, economics, world history, philosophy, and logic. However, partly as a result of this intense analytic training, Mill experienced a bout of depression in 1826. Some have called

---

[2]The abbreviation C.E. stands for ''Of the Common Era'' and replaces the more religiously biased convention A.D., which stands for ''Anno Domini,'' meaning ''in the year of our Lord.'' Similarly, B.C.E.—''Before the Common Era''—has replaced B.C., which means ''before Christ.''

this experience a "nervous breakdown." In his *Autobiography*, Mill himself characterizes the experience this way: "The habit of analysis has a tendency to wear away the feelings. . . . I was thus, as I said to myself, left stranded at the commencement of my voyage, with a well-equipped ship and a rudder, but no sail."[3] However, his emotional sails were partly filled by reading the Romantic poetry of Wordsworth. Mill's depression passed.

Certainly another emotional pivot was the woman in Mill's life, Harriet Taylor. She was married to a merchant, and Mill carried on a close friendship with her for twenty years until her husband's death. Then, in 1851, Mill and Harriet Taylor were married. She died just seven years later in 1858 while they were vacationing in France. Her body is buried in Avignon. Harriet Taylor's influence on John Stuart Mill's writing was enormous. His dedication page of the work, *On Liberty*, indicates the passion that Mill experienced with Taylor. "To the beloved and deplored memory of her who was the inspirer, and in part the author, of all that is best in my writings—the friend and wife whose exalted sense of truth and right was my strongest excitement . . . I dedicate this volume. Like all that I have written for many years, it belongs as much to her as to me . . ."[4]

Unlike many philosophers of the twentieth century, Mill never held a faculty appointment. He never taught at a university. To support himself, Mill worked as a clerk for the British East India Company beginning in 1823 and rising in its ranks until his retirement in 1858.

It should be noted that the England of Mill's time was experiencing the growth of both industrial and military power. Furthermore, the early experiments with democratic societies—specifically the United States—were becoming realities instead of remaining dreams in the minds of social reformers. Thus a major intellectual and practical concern of Mill's era was the proper organization and maintenance of society. Enveloped as he was in this historical arena, Mill was concerned with the place of women in society and the issue of slavery. His *The Subjection of Women*, published in 1869, demonstrates a sensitivity to those without power in society. His *On Liberty*, published in 1859, deals with the limits of a government's right to intervene in an individual's life. His *Principles of Political Economy*, published in 1848, also deals with social and economic issues. Even his *Autobiography*, published in 1873, highlights the possibilities of educational reform based on the experience of his own education. And Mill's passion for society and its proper ordering was not merely an intellectual activity. He served a brief term in Parliament from 1865 through 1868.

---

[3]John Stuart Mill, *Autobiography* (New York: Penguin, 1989), p. 115.
[4]John Stuart Mill, *On Liberty* (Indianapolis: Hackett, 1959), p. xxvi.

After a long career of asking, and answering, the tough questions in ethics and social theory, John Stuart Mill died in 1873.

Placing Mill's Thought in the History of Philosophy

When dealing with the question of ethics, philosophy can be divided into two major styles of thinking: *teleological* and *deontological*. Suppose you were thinking about cheating on an exam and decided that you should not do it because you could get caught and receive an F in the class. That style or way of thinking is considered teleological because it focuses on the *consequences* of an action to determine right and wrong. Suppose that your reason for not cheating was that cheating would be a violation of trust and your duty to your fellow classmates and school. This way of thinking is labeled deontological because it focuses on *duty* or *obligation* more than the consequences of actions. This distinction between teleological and deontological ethics does not necessarily determine different responses to a situation. It simply describes different ways of justifying one's actions. So teleological ethics focuses on consequences of actions; deontological ethics focuses on duty or obligation. Mill's *Utilitarianism* falls clearly within the tradition of teleological ethics.

To place Mill more clearly within this tradition of ethics, you should know that in the history of Western philosophy there is a long tradition of focusing on the consequences of an action to determine whether something is right or wrong. Ancient Greek philosophers, including Aristotle, can be placed within this tradition, which is called *teleological* because of its concern with the *ends* or *purpose* of an action (the Greek *telos* means *end* or *goal*). A key issue for any teleological approach to ethics is the question: What ends are worthy of being pursued? One answer that is common within the teleological tradition (but not the only possible answer) is that happiness or pleasure is the proper goal or end of all ethical action. This is called *hedonism*. A hedonist is a person whose criterion for judging the rightness or wrongness of behavior is the amount of pleasure that it produces. Hedonism's concern for pleasure is often complemented with a concern for avoiding pain. So hedonism is not necessarily a philosophy that justifies going to a party every night. That activity may produce some form of pain, which needs to be considered.

Jeremy Bentham, the English philosopher and social reformer of the eighteenth and nineteenth centuries, searched for a single ethical principle that could simplify and reform the country's legal system. Bentham's ''utility principle'' draws on the teleological tradition with pleasure or happiness as the criterion for ethical action. However, Bentham wished to broaden the philosophy of hedonism to include a social component. That is, Bentham wished to take the extent of happiness for a given society as the basis for ethics. He thought that pleasure was the proper criterion for right action, but he believed that everyone's pleasure or happiness should be taken into account. Ethics cannot be isolated from society as a whole.

In fact Bentham became famous for arguing that happiness and pleasure in a society could be measured quantitatively. A number could be assigned to a pleasure or a pain experienced by one person. Further, the quantity of pleasure would increase if that pleasure or happiness affected a great many people. After taking the extent of the happiness into account, a sum of the happiness or pleasure would tell anyone what the best action would be in any given situation. For example, if you were to eat an ice cream sundae, you would experience happiness or pleasure. But your four friends sitting next to you would not. If you shared your sundae, your pleasure would not be as great, but the pleasure would be distributed over a greater number of persons. The best action would be determined by the amount of happiness created by your eating the sundae by yourself and the amount of happiness or pleasure created by sharing the sundae with your friends. Whatever action would produce the greatest good for the greatest number of people would be the right thing to do. In this sense, ethics can be calculated, numerically, by fitting all the information into the equation.

Mill was greatly influenced by Bentham's ethical theories, but Mill was not satisfied with a purely quantitative approach. One of the most famous parts of *Utilitarianism* is the section where Mill adds a qualitative dimension to the principle of utility invoked by Bentham. Mill argues that some pleasures are of a qualitatively different kind. Mud wrestling is not the same as listening to Bach. No numerical distinction can describe the difference between making love and jogging. And where two pleasures *are* qualitatively different, who is to judge the right or the best one? For Mill, it is only ''competent judges'' who have experienced both, or all, the competing pleasures who can determine the right option. Which is better, mud wrestling or listening to Bach? Granting that these are qualitatively different pleasures or sources of happiness, only someone who has experienced both can judge.

So deeply is Mill rooted in the teleological approach to ethics that he argues forcefully against the style of ethical reflection that focuses on duty and obligation instead of the consequences of action. Thus the great eighteenth-century Prussian philosopher Immanuel Kant becomes Mill's philosophical adversary. In fact, in *Utilitarianism* Mill argues against Kant and the ''deontological'' (from the Greek *deontos* for duty) tradition of ethics. Kant's ''categorical imperative'' gives ethics a formula by which to decide right and wrong. In *Utilitarianism*, Mill even quotes Kant's famous assertion: ''So act that the rule on which thou actest would admit of being adopted as a law by all rational beings.''[5] Notice that this does not take into account the ends or consequences of any action. It merely describes an imperative, a law, a duty, an obligation that must be applied to any and all situations. But for Mill, even this deontological style of ethics can finally be reduced to his own version of utilitarianism.

So Mill's *Utilitarianism* is a form of consequentialism, a form of social hedonism, an ethical system that distinguishes itself within the teleological stream of ethics by recognizing a variety of *qualities* of pleasure or happiness, a theory that also defines itself as different from the deontological tradition of ethics.

A Summary of Utilitarianism

Chapter 1: General Remarks

Initially Mill is surprised that there is no consensus, and there has never been any real progress regarding the pivot point of ethics—''the criterion of right and wrong.'' Neither instinct nor intuition seem to produce an adequate criterion. So Mill says he will seek, in *Utilitarianism*, one fundamental principle or law at the root of morality.

For Mill the ethical principle that is most convincing is Bentham's principle of utility, the ''greatest happiness principle.'' This assertion, that the right or the good is produced by calculating the greatest good for the greatest number of people, informs all ethical reflection, even that of the opponents of utilitarianism. Mill mentions Immanuel Kant as one of these opponents and quickly argues that even Kant adheres to Bentham's principle of utility, though Kant would deny it.

How could Mill prove his argument? Mill admits that questions of ultimate ends cannot be proven directly; therefore direct, absolute proof is not available. However, there is a broader notion of proof, which is constructed by giving rational support for a conclusion. And it is this sort of proof, justification of a conclusion by reasons, that Mill will undertake in *Utilitarianism*.

Chapter 2: What Utilitarianism Is

In his second chapter, Mill begins to describe utilitarianism first by saying what it is not. Utilitarianism is not opposed to pleasure; it is not the same as bland ''usefulness'' or utility; and it is not equated

---

[5]John Stuart Mill & Jeremy Bentham, *Utilitarianism and Other Essays* (New York: Penguin, 1987), p. 275.

with the seeking of gross pleasure. Utilitarianism does have pleasure as a part of its formula. But Bentham included not only positive pleasure but also the absence of or exemption from pain. For utilitarianism, actions are right if they lead to happiness and wrong if they lead to the opposite of happiness. And for Mill, the only end or consequence desirable for humans is happiness.

In this chapter, however, Mill begins to differentiate his form of utilitarianism from that of Bentham. Whereas Bentham was quite content to measure and quantify pleasure and happiness, Mill thinks it necessary to include the notion of quality. That is, not all pleasures are alike. In fact, some pleasures are so different that they are *qualitatively different*. So pleasures cannot be measured on the same scale. Without this additional notion utilitarianism might be called ''piggish.'' For Mill, ''it is better to be a human being dissatisfied than a pig satisfied; better to be Socrates dissatisfied than a fool satisfied.'' And what happens when two pleasures of two different qualities are competing to distinguish right from wrong? Mill asserts that only ''competent judges,'' judges who have experienced all the different pleasures at issue, can distinguish right from wrong.

Mill then responds to the obvious experience of someone sacrificing his or her good for someone else. This in no way limits utilitarianism, says Mill; the greatest happiness principle even demands that such sacrifice be made. Mill's utilitarianism is not simply individualistic; it is not centered on the ego. This nineteenth-century form of utilitarianism is a form of social ethics. ''The greatest amount for the greatest number of people'' means that from time to time an individual must sacrifice his or her own good or interest for the greater good of the greater number of people. Mill concludes the chapter by answering the charges that utilitarianism is cold, godless, and merely expedient. Thus by defending utilitarianism against its detractors, Mill begins to describe and define his form of this ethical philosophy.

Chapter 3: Sanctions of the Principle of Utility

Every moral standard leads to the question: What is the source of obligation to obey this standard? This is true of any moral standard, not just the principle of utility. This question arises when we are asked to adopt a standard, especially one that is different from the one currently followed by our culture and society. In his third chapter Mill articulates both external and internal standards for the principle of utility. External standards are given and enforced by the culture, society, and God. Internal standards are those perceived to reside primarily with the individual, or ''conscience,'' rather than with society.

Chapter 4: Of What Sort of Proof the Principle of Utility Is Susceptible

In this short chapter Mill returns to an issue raised in the first chapter—the issue of proof and utilitarianism. Mill argues that the question of ultimate ends regarding ethics is really the question of what is desirable. Furthermore, Mill claims that happiness is the *only* thing desired by humans. What is the proof? For Mill, the proof is that people desire happiness and never desire anything else. Virtue, money, power, fame, and anything else one wanted to list would merely be means to happiness. And if they were so powerful as to be the end rather than the means, then they would be the same as happiness. "Happiness is the sole end of human action, and the promotion of it the test by which to judge of all human conduct. . . ." What about those acts of will that seem not informed by a desire for happiness? Mill asserts that the human will is "the child of desire," and ceases to be under the control of desire when formed into habit. Thus even acts of the will become subordinate to the desire for good. And "if this doctrine be true, the principle of utility is proved."

Chapter 5: On the Connection between Justice and Utility

This long and complicated last chapter responds to the common charge against any ethical theory that focuses on consequences. The charge is that *justice* is an inherent quality or criterion that is prior to or superior to any invocation of the principle of utility. Further, using justice as an ethical criterion is supposed to create clarity and simplicity in the moral life. But after analysis of the way justice is used in ethical theory, Mill is left not with clarity, but with confusion and contradictory views on the nature of justice. Supposedly, utilitarianism was the philosophy that led to uncertainty; justice was the certain criterion. Mill argues that this is not so. His conclusion: Justice itself is based on utility, the greatest happiness principle. "I account the justice which is grounded on utility to be the chief part, and incomparably the most sacred and binding part, of all morality." Thus, for Mill, the "only real difficulty" facing utilitarianism has been answered. The issue of ethics is resolved. The criterion for judging right and wrong is in place.

Reading Mill

Mill's prose in *Utilitarianism* was intended for a wide audience. *Utilitarianism* was first published as a series of articles in *Fraser's Magazine*, appearing between October and December of 1861. Mill's audience for *Utilitarianism* was not a graduate seminar in philosophy. Nor was it a class in the university. His audience was the general reading public of England in the middle of the nineteenth century. However, most contemporary American readers will find Mill's style dense and complicated.[6] One sentence in Chapter II has 168 words; even in small type, it takes up thirteen lines! Most of us are not accustomed to such intricate sentence structures. So how do you attempt to read John Stuart Mill? I will give one suggestion here at the beginning.[7] Then I will incorporate other suggestions for reading Mill as we go along.

When you look at all the words of a sentence and have no clue about what that sentence means, stop. *Do not* get angry or frustrated. Simply stop. Then ask yourself this question: "What is happening in this sentence?" Look at the sentence again and decide what is happening. (English professors call this task *locating the verb.* I do not care what it is called; it is only important here that you discover what is happening.) Then underline what is happening, in red if you have a red pen or pencil or in regular pencil if you do not. For example, what is happening in the sentence "The dog ate the cat."? Isn't it true that eating is what is happening? So underline *ate.* Let's take another simple example. In "The dog was surprised by the cat," being surprised is happening. So underline *was surprised.* Philosophical writing is often more difficult than these two simple examples. Often what is happening is a mental operation. For example, in "Kant was concerned with ethics," being concerned is what is happening. That is a mental action. In "To many, Mill appears an introvert," appearing is happening. Again, this is not overt, physical activity. It is more mental; remember that the action in a sentence can deal with ideas.

When you are satisfied that you have figured out what is happening in the sentence, you can move on to the second step in this process. Ask yourself, "Who or what is _____?" In the space, place your answer to the first question. Here you are trying to figure out the person or the thing that is doing the action. (English instructors call this the *subject.*) In my examples above, who or what was surprised? The dog was surprised. Who or what is eating? The dog is eating. Who or what was concerned? Kant was

---

[6]Alan Ryan, a noted commentator on Mill's writing, says that "Since it [*Utilitarianism*] is short, readable, polemical and eloquent, it has always offered an easy way into the complexities of moral philosophy and into the creed of the utilitarian movement." My experience, however, is that reading Mill is difficult. Further, a readability analysis of the first paragraph of *Utilitarianism* yields a Flesch Reading Ease score of 4.0 (Very difficult). The reading grade level for that score is 16. This would suggest that only approximately 5 percent of U.S. adults would be able to read the selection easily. [Ryan's quote is found in John Stuart Mill & Jeremy Bentham, *Utilitarianism and Other Essays* (New York: Penguin, 1987), p. 7.]

[7] I would like to thank my colleague, Kay Weiss, a professor whose academic specialty is reading theory, for this suggestion.

concerned. Who or what appeared? Mill appeared. Underline your answer to this question in blue if you have a blue pencil or pen. If you do not, underline the answer to this question with a "squiggly" line to differentiate it from the line under the action of the sentence.

Once you have found the answer to these two questions and underlined them, you have visually identified the building blocks of the sentence: the verb and the subject. Everything else in the sentence merely expands or qualifies these two key ingredients. Knowing this, even Mill's lengthy sentences can be broken down into smaller components. Initially you can ignore the rest of his sentence (usually sets of words enclosed by commas), and then as you read the sentence again, each time you can add another one of those qualifications. This reinforces the central meaning of the sentence and allows you to figure out what is going on in the entire sentence.

Let us take an example from the first paragraph of *Utilitarianism.* "From the dawn of philosophy, the question concerning the *summum bonum,* or, what is the same thing, concerning the foundation of morality, has been accounted the main problem in speculative thought, has occupied the most gifted intellects and divided them into sects and schools carrying on a vigorous warfare against one another." This is a long sentence! Probably its meanings are not quickly apparent. So stop. Do not despair. Slow down and take the sentence apart. If this sentence is not a problem for you, and if the meanings are quickly apparent, that is wonderful. However, this technique may help you if you are ever puzzled in your reading.

First ask "What is happening?" Take the first phrase, "From the dawn of philosophy." Is there anything happening there? No. This is just a phrase referring to time. Take the next segment, "the question concerning the *summum bonum,* or, what is the same thing, concerning the foundation of morality." Anything happening there? Not yet. Take the next phrase, "has been accounted the main problem in speculative thought." Anything happening here? Yes! This is not obvious physical activity like swimming or skiing, but something "has been accounted." What is happening? Taking account is happening. In other words something has been noticed or brought to mind. Notice how you can use other words to help explain what might not be clear initially. So you have begun to answer the question, "What is happening?" Underline *has been accounted* in red or plain pencil. Is anything else happening? The next phrase, "has occupied the most gifted intellects," also suggests that something is happening. Occupying is happening. So underline *has occupied* also. Is anything else happening? Yes. Something has "divided them into sects and schools." Division is happening. Underline this phrase as well.

So, three things are happening in this sentence. What are they? First, "accounting" or "taking acount" is happening. Also _____ and _____ are happening. It is important that you underline these in red or with a straight line in the example. The underlining gives you a visual clue to use when you reconstruct the sentence.

Then ask "Who or what has been accounted? Who or what is occupying? Who or what is dividing?" Go through the parts of the sentence again. Is "From the dawn of philosophy" the answer to "Who or what was taken into account?" No. What about "the question concerning the *summum bonum?*" Is that the answer to "Who or what is taken into account? Yes! "The question" has been accounted. You will quickly see that "the question" is also what is doing the occupying. Furthermore, that same question is also dividing. Underline *the question* in blue or with a squiggly line in plain pencil. Now you have identified the basics of the sentence.

Then you ask, "What sort of question is accounting and occupying and dividing?" The question of the *summum bonum* (the foundation of morality) is occupying and accounting and dividing. Occupying what or accounting for what? The question of the foundation of morality has been accounted the main problem and has occupied people with gifted intellects. Anything else? The question of the foundation of morality (the *summum bonum*) has been the main problem in speculative thought since the beginning of philosophy; this problem has occupied smart people and divided them against each other.

This was a very difficult sentence. But with this suggestion for reading, you have paraphrased or translated Mill's language into your own. You began with the action and with the thing or person doing the action, then you added to the meaning of the sentence by adding qualifying phrases and clauses. If you follow this pattern, you will have a greater understanding of Mill's philosophy. Like any technique, this takes practice. And this technique works best when you have a reading partner, a study group, or class time to work out the problems with others who are struggling with the same very difficult reading. You can read philosophy by yourself, but try reading with someone else. Or at least have someone you can be with when the going gets tough.

Now let's see how this sentence might look in your book after you have used this reading technique. "From the dawn of philosophy, the question concerning the *summum bonum,* or, what is the same thing, concerning the foundation of morality, has been accounted the main problem in speculative thought, has occupied the most gifted intellects and divided them into sects and schools carrying on a vigorous warfare against one another." Of course you don't do this process with every sentence. It works best when you are very confused and need to slow down and investigate the language. You will encounter these other ways to help yourself understand Mill as you go through this text.

Now that you have read this introduction, your guided tour will begin. But first, let's review. The primary goal of this introduction was to tell you the question underlying *Utilitarianism*.

The underlying concern or question of *Utilitarianism* is _____

_____ .

This introduction was also supposed to tell something about Mill's life and times.
The first thing you remember about Mill's life is _____

_____

_____ .

Why is this important to you or to your understanding of Mill?

It is important because _____

_____ .

What else do you remember about Mill's life?

I remember _____

_____ .

This is important because _____

_____ .

What is the first thing that you remember about the history and culture within which Mill writes?

I remember _____

_____ .

What else do you remember about the social setting of Mill's philosophy?

I remember _____ .
Finally the introduction was to place Mill's work within the history of philosophy.
Utilitarianism is similar to previous philosophies in the way that

it deals with _____

_____

_____ .

Mill's thought differs from previous philosophies in the way that

it deals with _____ .

From the summary of *Utilitarianism,* what is the first thing you remember?

I remember _____.

What else do you remember from the summary?

I remember _____

_____.

Finally, when your reading gets stuck, you stop and ask yourself what question first?

The first question I ask is ''What is _____?''

Then you ask what question?

I ask ''_____

_____?''

Your active reading has begun. Bon voyage!

PART 2
John Stuart Mill's Utilitarianism

Chapter 1
General Remarks

Initially Mill is surprised that there is no consensus and has never been any real progress regarding the pivot point of ethics: ''the criterion of right and wrong.'' So Mill will seek, in *Utilitarianism*, one fundamental principle or law at the root of morality. For Mill, the ethical principle that is most convincing is Bentham's principle of utility, the ''greatest happiness principle.'' This assertion, that the right or the good is produced by calculating the greatest good for the greatest number of people, informs all ethical reflection. How could Mill prove his argument? Mill believes that one can construct a broad notion of proof by giving rational support for a conclusion. And it is this sort of proof, justification of a conclusion by reasons, that Mill will undertake in *Utilitarianism*.

Mill says that little progress has been made regarding the question of _____ , or, to put it another way, the issue of the foundation of _____ _____ .

There are few circumstances among those which make up the present condition of human knowledge, more unlike what might have been expected, or more significant of the backward state in which speculation on the most important subjects still lingers, than the little progress which has been made in the decision of the controversy respecting the criterion of right and wrong. From the dawn of philosophy, the question concerning the *summum bonum*,[1] or, what is the same thing, concerning the foundation of morality, has been accounted the main problem in speculative thought, has occupied the most gifted intellects, and divided them into sects and schools, carrying on a vigorous warfare against one another. And after more than two thousand years the same discussions continue,

1

philosophers are still ranged under the same contending banners, and neither thinkers nor mankind at large seem nearer to being unanimous on the subject, than when the youth *Socrates*[2] listened to the old *Protagoras*,[3] and asserted (if *Plato's*[4] dialogue be grounded on a real conversation) the theory of utilitarianism against the popular morality of the so-called *sophist*.[5]

It is true that similar confusion and uncertainty, and in some cases similar discordance, exist respecting the first principles of all the sciences, not excepting that which is deemed the most certain of them, mathematics; without much impairing, generally indeed without impairing at all, the trustworthiness of the conclusions of those sciences. An apparent anomaly, the explanation of which is, that the detailed doctrines of a science are not usually deduced from, nor depend for their evidence upon, what are called its first principles. Were it not so, there would be no science more precarious, or whose conclusions were more insufficiently made out, than algebra; which derives none of its certainty from what are commonly taught to learners as its elements, since these, as laid down by some of its most eminent teachers, are as full of fictions as English law, and of mysteries as theology. The truths which are ultimately accepted as the first principles of a science, are really the last results of metaphysical analysis, practised on the elementary notions with which the science is conversant; and their relation to the science is not that of foundations to an edifice, but of roots to a tree, which may perform their office equally well though they be never dug down to and exposed to light. But though in science the particular truths precede the general theory, the contrary might be expected to be the case with a practical art, such as morals or legislation. All action is for the sake of some end, and rules of action, it seems natural to suppose, must take their whole character and colour from the end to which they are subservient. When we engage in a pursuit, a clear and precise conception of what we are pursuing would seem to be the first thing we need, instead of the last we are to look forward to. A test of right and wrong must be the means, one would think, of ascertaining what is right or wrong, and not a consequence of having already ascertained it.

The difficulty is not avoided by having recourse to the popular theory of a natural faculty, a sense or instinct, informing us of right and wrong. For—besides that the existence of such a moral instinct is itself one of the matters in dispute—those believers in it who have any pretensions to philosophy, have been obliged to abandon the idea that it discerns what is right or wrong in the particular case in hand, as our other senses discern the sight or sound actually present. Our moral faculty, according to all those of its interpreters who are entitled to the name of thinkers, supplies us only with the general principles of moral judgments; it is a branch of our reason,

2

In morals and legislation, which comes first for Mill, particular

truths or general theory? _____

_____ .

Underline the last sentence in this paragraph. It will be important when you review the highlights of this chapter.

3

not of our sensitive faculty; and must be looked to for the abstract doctrines of morality, not for perception of it in the concrete. The intuitive, no less than what may be termed the inductive, school of ethics, insists on the necessity of general laws. They both agree that the morality of an individual action is not a question of direct perception, but of the application of a law to an individual case. They recognize also, to a great extent, the same moral laws; but differ as to their evidence, and the source from which they derive their authority. According to the one opinion, the principles of morals are evident *à priori*,[6] requiring nothing to command assent, except that the meaning of the terms be understood. According to the other doctrine, right and wrong, as well as truth and falsehood, are questions of observation and experience. But both hold equally that morality must be deduced from principles; and the intuitive school affirm as strongly as the inductive, that there is a science of morals. Yet they seldom attempt to make out a list of the *à priori* principles which are to serve as the premises of the science; still more rarely do they make any effort to reduce those various principles to one first principle, or common ground of obligation. They either assume the ordinary precepts of morals as of *à priori* authority, or they lay down as the common groundwork of those maxims, some generality much less obviously authoritative than the maxims themselves, and which has never succeeded in gaining popular acceptance. Yet to support their pretensions there ought either to be some one fundamental principle or law, at the root of all morality, or if there be several, there should be a determinate order of precedence among them; and the one principle, or the rule for deciding between the various principles when they conflict, ought to be self-evident.

The most important idea in this paragraph is _____ _____.

To inquire how far the bad effects of this deficiency have been   4
mitigated in practice, or to what extent the moral beliefs of mankind have been vitiated or made uncertain by the absence of any distinct recognition of an ultimate standard, would imply a complete survey and criticism of past and present ethical doctrine. It would, however, be easy to show that whatever steadiness or consistency these moral beliefs have attained, has been mainly due to the tacit influence of a standard not recognized. Although the nonexistence of an acknowledged first principle has made ethics not so much a guide as a consecration of men's actual sentiments, still, as men's sentiments, both of favor and of aversion, are greatly influenced by what they suppose to be the effects of things upon their happiness, the principle of utility, or as *Bentham*[7] latterly called it, the greatest happiness principle, has had a large share in forming the moral doctrines even of those who most scornfully reject its authority. Nor is there any school of thought which refuses to admit that the influence of actions on happiness is a most material and even predominant

consideration in many of the details of morals, however unwilling to acknowledge it as the fundamental principle of morality, and the source of moral obligation. I might go much further, and say that to all those *à priori* moralists who deem it necessary to argue at all, utilitarian arguments are indispensable. It is not my present purpose to criticize these thinkers; but I cannot help referring, for illustration, to a systematic treatise by one of the most illustrious of them, the *Metaphysics of Ethics, by Kant.*[8] This remarkable man, whose system of thought will long remain one of the landmarks in the history of philosophical speculation, does, in the treatise in question, lay down an universal first principle as the origin and ground of moral obligation; it is this:—''So act, that the rule on which thou attest would admit of being adopted as a law by all rational beings.'' But when he begins to deduce from this precept any of the actual duties of morality, he fails, almost grotesquely, to show that there would be any contradiction, any logical (not to say physical) impossibility, in the adoption by all rational beings of the most outrageously immoral rules of conduct. All he shows is that the *consequences* of their universal adoption would be such as no one would choose to incur.

On the present occasion, I shall, without further discussion of the other theories, attempt to contribute something towards the understanding and appreciation of the Utilitarian or Happiness theory, and towards such proof as it is susceptible of. It is evident that this cannot be proof in the ordinary and popular meaning of the term. Questions of ultimate ends are not amenable to direct proof. Whatever can be proved to be good, must be so by being shown to be a means to something admitted to be good without proof. The medical art is proved to be good, by its conducing to health; but how is it possible to prove that health is good? The art of music is good, for the reason, among others, that it produces pleasure; but what proof is it possible to give that pleasure is good? If, then, it is asserted that there is a comprehensive formula, including all things which are in themselves good, and that whatever else is good, is not so as an end, but as a mean*, the formula may be accepted or rejected, but is not a subject of what is commonly understood by proof. We are not, however, to infer that its acceptance or rejection must depend on blind impulse, or arbitrary choice. There is a larger meaning of the word proof, in which this question is as amenable to it as any other of the disputed questions of philosophy. The subject is within the cognizance of the rational faculty; and neither does that faculty deal with it solely in the way of intuition. Considerations may be presented capable of determining the

---

*means

The moral standard that Mill says has always been operating tacitly in ethics, even when rejected by its

opponent, is _____

_____ .

Underline Kant's ''principle of moral obligation.'' Kant calls this ''the categorical imperative,'' and it represents a style of thinking very different from Mill's.

5

What are the two meanings of *proof* in this paragraph?

The first is _____

_____ .

The second meaning of *proof* is ___

_____ .

intellect either to give or withhold its assent to the doctrine; and this is equivalent to proof.

We shall examine presently of what nature are these considerations; in what manner they apply to the case, and what rational grounds therefore, can be given for accepting or rejecting the utilitarian formula. But it is a preliminary condition of rational acceptance or rejection, that the formula should be correctly understood. I believe that the very imperfect notion ordinarily formed of its meaning, is the chief obstacle which impedes its reception; and that could it be cleared, even from only the grosser misconceptions, the question would be greatly simplified, and a large proportion of its difficulties removed. Before, therefore, I attempt to enter into the philosophical grounds which can be given for assenting to the utilitarian standard, I shall offer some illustrations of the doctrine itself; with the view of showing more clearly what it is, distinguishing it from what it is not, and disposing of such of the practical objections to it as either originate in, or are closely connected with, mistaken interpretations of its meaning. Having thus prepared the ground, I shall afterwards endeavor to throw such light as I can upon the question, considered as one of philosophical theory.

Underline what Mill says is the chief obstacle to understanding utilitarianism. Here Mill gives you a hint about what will be coming in the next chapter.

Sometimes it is helpful to summarize a chapter or a section of philosophical writing by identifying the main ideas or the key points in each paragraph. You can do this by writing a word, a short phrase, or even a sentence for each paragraph in the text. This probably means that you will have to look again, quickly, at each paragraph in succession. That's OK. It is a good way to review. Let's try this with Chapter 1.

In paragraph 1, Mill's main idea is that there is still confusion over the issue of the foundation of _____. Mill is saying in paragraph 2 that a first principle or foundation of morality is necessary. Paragraph 3 still concerns itself with the foundation of _____. In paragraph 4, Mill argues against Kant and his ''categorical imperative'' and says that there is a first principle for morality, the principle of _____, or what Bentham called the ''greatest _____ principle.'' Speaking about the nature of _____ in paragraph 5, Mill says that by ''_____'' he means giving of reasons, not demonstrating that something necessarily exists. Concluding the chapter in paragraph 6, Mill's main point is to clarify what is _____ and to distinguish

utilitarianism from _____.

Now you have summarized or paraphrased—put in your own words—the ideas of John Stuart Mill. Now ask yourself this question: "How do *I* know right from wrong?" Try to write one sentence that could explain why *you* know when some action is right or wrong.

"I can tell right from wrong by _____

_____.

Would Mill agree with you? _____ You will be better able to answer this question at the end of *Utilitarianism,* but you should at least attempt an answer at this point. No matter what you just said, be open to the possibility that your understanding of Mill will change, or that *your* ideas might change.

Mill says in paragraph 1 that the issue of ethics and how people know right and wrong continues to be a source of disagreement. Have you ever disagreed with someone on an ethical issue? We assume that you have. Why do you think there was a difference of opinion?

There was a difference because _____

_____.

The principle of utility mentioned in paragraph 4 will be key in Mill's thinking. This principle is called "the greatest happiness principle." For Mill, the greatest happiness principle means

_____

_____.

Now that you have summarized, clarified, and begun to converse with the writing of John Stuart Mill, what next? Reread paragraph 6 and see if Mill gives you any hints. Mill's first task in the next chapter will be to _____

_____.

Notes

1. *Summum bonum* is a Latin phrase meaning "the highest good."

2. Socrates (469–399 B.C.E.) was the teacher of Plato, and was famous for his constant questioning of "people in the know." Although he wrote nothing, his influence on the style of

Western philosophy is felt through his constant asking of questions, as reported by Plato.

3. Protagoras lived ca. 450 B.C.E. and was a Greek philosopher who argued that there is no single absolute truth and that ''man is the measure''—that is, humanity is the yardstick for knowledge and reality. Plato wrote a dialogue with this name as the title. One of the characters in that dialogue is named Protagoras.

4. Plato (427–347 B.C.E.) was a student of Socrates and is considered the first great ''systematic'' philosopher in the West. He wrote his philosophical ideas in the form of dialogues, and Socrates is often a character in these dialogues.

5. The Sophists were teachers in the fifth and fourth centuries B.C.E. in Greece. Sophists were the recipients of much of Plato's and Socrates' philosophic wrath. Trained in rhetoric and public speaking, Plato and Socrates thought that these ''wise men'' merely pretended to teach knowledge.

6. The Latin phrase *a priori* has come to mean philosophically ''prior to sense experience.''

7. Jeremy Bentham (1748–1832 C.E.) was a British social reformer and philosopher. He was close to the family of John Stuart Mill. See the Introduction for more information on Bentham.

8. Immanuel Kant (1724–1804 C.E.) was a Prussian philosopher famous for his deontological approach to ethics. See the Introduction for more information on deontology. Kant's ''categorical imperative''—act so that the maxim for your actions can be universalized—provided Mill with an opposing viewpoint on ethics.

Chapter 2
What Utilitarianism Is

In this second chapter, Mill begins to describe utilitarianism first by saying what it is not. Utilitarianism is not opposed to pleasure; it is not the same as bland ''usefulness,'' or utility; and it is not to be equated with the seeking of gross pleasure. Utilitarianism does have pleasure as a part of its formula. But Bentham included not only positive pleasure but also the absence of or exemption from pain. For utilitarianism, actions are right if they lead to happiness, wrong if they lead to the opposite of happiness. And for Mill the only end or consequence desirable for humans is happiness.

In this chapter, however, Mill begins to differentiate his form of utilitarianism from that of Bentham. Whereas Bentham was quite content to measure and quantify pleasure and happiness, Mill thinks it necessary to include the notion of quality. That is, not all pleasures are alike. In fact, some pleasures are so different that they are *qualitatively different.* So not all pleasures can be measured on the same scale. And what happens when two pleasures of two different qualities are competing to distinguish right from wrong? Mill asserts that only ''competent judges,'' judges who have experienced all the different pleasures at issue, can distinguish right from wrong.

Mill then responds to the obvious experience of someone sacrificing his or her good for someone else. Indeed the greatest happiness principle demands such sacrifices. Mill's utilitarianism is not individualistic; it is not centered on the ego. This nineteenth-century form of utilitarianism is a form of social ethics.

"The greatest amount for the greatest number of people" means that from time to time an individual must sacrifice his or her own good or interest for the greater good of the greater number of people.

In this paragraph, mark in the margin every time Mill tells how the word *utility* has been misused.

The first "blunder" is that utility is thought to be _____ to pleasure. This means that for Mill, utilitarianism is not _____ .

The next charge against utilitarianism is that it refers everything merely to the grossest form of

_____ .

Underline the sentence beginning "Those who know. . . ." Here Mill locates within the history of philosophy his ideas about pleasure.

But for Epicurus and Bentham, utility meant pleasure together with _____ .

A passing remark is all that needs to be given to the ignorant blunder of supposing that those who stand up for utility as the test of right and wrong, use the term in that restricted and merely colloquial sense in which utility is opposed to pleasure. An apology is due to the philosophical opponents of utilitarianism, for even the momentary appearance of confounding them with anyone capable of so absurd a misconception; which is the more extraordinary, inasmuch as the contrary accusation, of referring everything to pleasure, and that too in its grossest form, is another of the common charges against utilitarianism: and, as has been pointedly remarked by an able writer, the same sort of persons, and often the very same persons, denounce the theory "as impracticably dry when the word utility precedes the word pleasure, and as too practicably voluptuous when the word pleasure precedes the word utility." Those who know anything about the matter are aware that every writer, from Epicurus[1] to Bentham, who maintained the theory of utility, meant by it, not something to be contradistinguished from pleasure, but pleasure itself, together with exemption from pain; and instead of opposing the useful to the agreeable or the ornamental, have always declared that the useful means these, among other things. Yet the common herd, including the herd of writers, not only in newspapers and periodicals, but in books of weight and pretension, are perpetually falling into this shallow mistake. Having caught up the word utilitarian, while knowing nothing whatever about it but its sound, they habitually express by it the rejection, or the neglect, of pleasure in some of its forms; of beauty, of ornament, or of amusement. Nor is the term thus ignorantly misapplied solely in disparagement, but occasionally, in compliment; as though it implied superiority to frivolity and the mere pleasures of the moment. And this perverted use is the only one in which the word is popularly known, and the one from which the new generation are acquiring their sole notion of its meaning. Those who introduced the word, but who had for many years discontinued it as a distinctive appellation, may well feel themselves called upon to resume it, if by doing so they can hope to contribute anything towards rescuing it from this utter degradation.*

1

---

*The author of this essay has reason for believing himself to be the first person who brought the word utilitarianism into use. He did not invent it, but adopted it from a passing expression in Mr. [John] Galt's *Annals of the Parish* [Edinburgh: Blackwood,

The creed which accepts as the foundation of morals, Utility, or the Greatest Happiness Principle, holds that actions are right in proportion as they tend to promote happiness, wrong as they tend to produce the reverse of happiness. By happiness is intended pleasure, and the absence of pain; by unhappiness, pain, and the privation of pleasure. To give a clear view of the moral standard set up by the theory, much more requires to be said; in particular, what things it includes in the ideas of pain and pleasure; and to what extent this is left an open question. But these supplementary explanations do not affect the theory of life on which this theory of morality is grounded—namely, that pleasure, and freedom from pain, are the only things desirable as ends; and that all desirable things (which are as numerous in the utilitarian as in any other scheme) are desirable either for the pleasure inherent in themselves, or as means to the promotion of pleasure and the prevention of pain.

2
This is an important paragraph. Read it slowly and carefully.

Underline the first sentence of this paragraph and circle the phrase "the Greatest Happiness Principle." This will be a reference point as you review.

Underline the two things—the only two things, according to Mill—that are desirable as ends.

Since this second chapter is rather long, let's stop here and reflect on the reading. In the first paragraph, Mill is telling you what utilitarianism is by beginning to list some of the misconceptions about it. The two "blunders" or misconceptions about utilitarianism that you remember from paragraph 1 is that utilitarianism

was thought to be _____ and that utilitarianism was thought to be _____ .

In the second paragraph, Mill makes it clear what the foundation of morality is—the principle of utility or, what is the same thing for Mill, the greatest happiness principle. The principle of utility is the principle that _____

_____ or that _____ is the criterion for right and wrong action.

Imagine that John Stuart Mill is sitting with you right now. If he were present, what question would you want to ask him at this point in your reading?

I would like to ask _____

_____

_____ .

1821, p. 286]. After using it as a designation for several years, he and others abandoned it from a growing dislike to anything resembling a badge or watchword of sectarian distinction. But as a name for one single opinion, not a set of opinions—to denote the recognition of utility as a [61 the] standard, not any particular way of applying it—the term supplies a want in the language, and offers, in many cases, a convenient mode of avoiding tiresome circumlocution.

I would want to know this because _____

_____

_____ .

If while you read other questions arise that you would like to ask Mill, write them in the margins of your text. Your questions then become the basis for your reading and your understanding of Mill's ideas.

Now, such a theory of life excites in many minds, and among them in some of the most estimable in feeling and purpose, inveterate dislike. To suppose that life has (as they express it) no higher end than pleasure—no better and nobler object of desire and pursuit—they designate as utterly mean and grovelling; as a doctrine worthy only of swine, to whom the followers of Epicurus were, at a very early period, contemptuously likened; and modern holders of the doctrine are occasionally made the subject of equally polite comparisons by its German, French, and English assailants. 3

When thus attacked, the Epicureans have always answered, that it is not they, but their accusers, who represent human nature in a degrading light; since the accusation supposes human beings to be capable of no pleasures except those of which swine are capable. If this supposition were true, the charge could not be gainsaid, but would then be no longer an imputation; for if the sources of pleasure were precisely the same to human beings and to swine, the rule of life which is good enough for the one would be good enough for the other. The comparison of the Epicurean life to that of beasts is felt as degrading, precisely because a beast's pleasures do not satisfy a human being's conceptions of happiness. Human beings have faculties more elevated than the animal appetites, and when once made conscious of them, do not regard anything as happiness which does not include their gratification. I do not, indeed, consider the Epicureans to have been by any means faultless in drawing out their scheme of consequences from the utilitarian principle. To do this in any sufficient manner, many Stoic,[2] as well as Christian elements require to be included. But there is no known Epicurean theory of life which does not assign to the pleasures of the intellect, of the feelings and imagination, and of the moral sentiments, a much higher value as pleasures than to those of mere sensation. It must be admitted, however, that utilitarian writers in general have placed the superiority of mental over bodily pleasures chiefly in the greater permanency, safety, uncostliness, etc. of the former—that is, in their circumstantial advantages rather than in their intrinsic nature. And on all these points utilitarians have fully proved their case; but they might have taken the other, and, as it may be called, higher ground, 4

What pleasures besides physical pleasures does Epicurus's theory include?

Circle the words *quality* and *quantity* in the next three paragraphs. They are important because Mill's emphasis on quality is what makes his ideas in *Utilitarianism* unique.

with entire consistency. It is quite compatible with the principle of utility to recognize the fact, that some *kinds* of pleasure are more desirable and more valuable than others. It would be absurd that while, in estimating all other things, quality is considered as well as quantity, the estimation of pleasures should be supposed to depend on quantity alone.

Underline the last sentence of this paragraph. Mill clearly states that quality is an important consideration.

If I am asked, what I mean by difference of quality in pleasures, or what makes one pleasure more valuable than another, merely as a pleasure, except its being greater in amount, there is but one possible answer. Of two pleasures, if there be one to which all or almost all who have experience of both give a decided preference, irrespective of any feeling of moral obligation to prefer it, that is the more desirable pleasure. If one of the two is, by those who are competently acquainted with both, placed so far above the other that they prefer it, even though knowing it to be attended with a greater amount of discontent, and would not resign it for any quantity of the other pleasure which their nature is capable of, we are justified in ascribing to the preferred enjoyment a superiority in quality, so far outweighing quantity as to render it, in comparison, of small account.

5

Who would be capable of judging between two competing pleasures? Mill would say someone who has

_____.

Now it is an unquestionable fact that those who are equally acquainted with, and equally capable of appreciating and enjoying, both, do give a most marked preference to the manner of existence which employs their higher faculties. Few human creatures would consent to be changed into any of the lower animals, for a promise of the fullest allowance of a beast's pleasures; no intelligent human being would consent to be a fool, no instructed person would be an ignoramus, no person of feeling and conscience would be selfish and base, even though they should be persuaded that the fool, the dunce, or the rascal is better satisfied with his lot than they are with theirs. They would not resign what they possess more than he, for the most complete satisfaction of all the desires which they have in common with him. If they ever fancy they would, it is only in cases of unhappiness so extreme, that to escape from it they would exchange their lot for almost any other, however undesirable in their own eyes. A being of higher faculties requires more to make him happy, is capable probably of more acute suffering, and is certainly accessible to it at more points, than one of an inferior type; but in spite of these liabilities, he can never really wish to sink into what he feels to be a lower grade of existence. We may give what explanation we please of this unwillingness; we may attribute it to pride, a name which is given indiscriminately to some of the most and to some of the least estimable feelings of which mankind are capable; we may refer it to the love of liberty and personal independence, an appeal to which was with the Stoics one of the most effective means for the inculcation of it; to the love of power, or to the love

6

From Mill's discussion, what do you think he thinks some of the "higher faculties" are? I think some of the higher faculties are

_____.

Do you agree with Mill on this "unquestionable fact" about the

higher faculties? _____.

Mill gives five explanations for not wanting to sink to lower levels of existence. They are: (1) pride;

(2) _____ ;

(3) _____ ;

(4) _____ ;

and (5) dignity.

Underline the rest of this paragraph. It is one of the most quoted sections of *Utilitarianism*.

of excitement, both of which do really enter into and contribute to it: but its most appropriate appellation is a sense of dignity, which all human beings possess in one form or other, and in some, though by no means in exact, proportion to their higher faculties, and which is so essential a part of the happiness of those in whom it is strong, that nothing which conflicts with it could be, otherwise than momentarily, an object of desire to them. Whoever supposes that this preference takes place at a sacrifice of happiness—that the superior being, in anything like equal circumstances, is not happier than the inferior—confounds the two very different ideas, of happiness, and content. It is indisputable that the being whose capacities of enjoyment are low, has the greatest chance of having them fully satisfied; and a highly-endowed being will always feel that any happiness which he can look for, as the world is constituted, is imperfect. But he can learn to bear its imperfections, if they are at all bearable; and they will not make him envy the being who is indeed unconscious of the imperfections, but only because he feels not at all the good which those imperfections qualify. It is better to be a human being dissatisfied than a pig satisfied; better to be Socrates dissatisfied than a fool satisfied. And if the fool, or the pig, is of a different opinion, it is because they only know their own side of the question. The other party to the comparison knows both sides.

The criterion for right and wrong actions is the greatest happiness principle—the right thing to do creates the greatest amount of happiness for the greatest number of people. But Mill has added the notion of quality to this utilitarian equation. So that you can better understand the difference between quantity and quality, write down three things that are pleasurable and rank them on a scale of 1–10, with 10 being the most pleasurable. Two examples are given for you.

Eating ice cream	5
Winning the lottery	8
_____	__
_____	__
_____	__

Now write down something pleasurable or happy that is qualitatively different from the three pleasures that you just listed, something that is so completely out of the range of values that it cannot be put in the same list.

_____

_____

Was this difficult for you to do? The difference between quantity and quality is very important in Mill's version of utilitarianism. But does it make sense to you to use this distinction? That is, is it important for you in deciding what is right and wrong to understand the difference between quality and quantity? Certainly your ideas will change as you read, but what is your reaction to this at this point?

I think that Mill's ideas about quality are _____ important in deciding right from wrong. I say this because _____

_____

_____

_____

_____.

The "only competent judges" for those pleasures that are qualitatively different are people who have experienced both or all the competing pleasures. Go back to your list above. Who would be a competent judge for that list? Who has experienced them all? You may list individuals or groups if necessary.

_____

_____

_____

Imagine that you are talking with your best friend. She (or he) asks you to tell her (or him) about your studies. Try to paraphrase for her the last three sentences of paragraph 6. Mill says that it is better to be a human being dissatisfied than a

_____ satisfied; better to be _____

dissatisfied than a fool _____. What Mill is saying here is _____

_____

_____

_____.

Now your friend asks you, "Why is that important?" Good question! It is important because _____

_____

_____

_____.

The objection to Mill's position that he responds to here is that people occasionally postpone the _____ pleasures to the _____ pleasures.

Capacities for higher, nobler feelings can be destroyed by _____ and by _____ .

The essential characteristic of a "competent judge" is _____ _____ .

It may be objected, that many who are capable of the higher pleasures, occasionally, under the influence of temptation, postpone them to the lower. But this is quite compatible with a full appreciation of the intrinsic superiority of the higher. Men often, from infirmity of character, make their election for the nearer good, though they know it to be the less valuable; and this no less when the choice is between two bodily pleasures, than when it is between bodily and mental. They pursue sensual indulgences to the injury of health, though perfectly aware that health is the greater good. It may be further objected, that many who begin with youthful enthusiasm for everything noble, as they advance in years sink into indolence and selfishness. But I do not believe that those who undergo this very common change, voluntarily choose the lower description of pleasures in preference to the higher. I believe that before they devote themselves exclusively to the one, they have already become incapable of the other. Capacity for the nobler feelings is in most natures a very tender plant, easily killed, not only by hostile influences, but by mere want of sustenance; and in the majority of young persons it speedily dies away if the occupations to which their position in life has devoted them, and the society into which it has thrown them, are not favorable to keeping that higher capacity in exercise. Men lose their high aspirations as they lose their intellectual tastes, because they have not time or opportunity for indulging them; and they addict themselves to inferior pleasures, not because they deliberately prefer them, but because they are either the only ones to which they have access, or the only ones which they are any longer capable of enjoying. It may be questioned whether anyone who has remained equally susceptible to both classes of pleasures, ever knowingly and calmly preferred the lower; though many, in all ages, have broken down in an ineffectual attempt to combine both.

From this verdict of the only competent judges, I apprehend there can be no appeal. On a question which is the best worth having of two pleasures, or which of two modes of existence is the most grateful to the feelings, apart from its moral attributes and from its consequences, the judgment of those who are qualified by knowledge of both, or, if they differ, that of the majority among them, must be admitted as final. And there needs be the less hesitation to accept this judgment respecting the quality of pleasures, since there is no other tribunal to be referred to even on the question of quantity. What means are there of determining which is the acutest of two pains, or the intensest of two pleasurable sensations, except the general suffrage of those who are familiar with both? Neither pains nor pleasures are homogeneous, and pain is always heterogeneous with pleasure. What is there to decide whether a particular pleasure is worth purchasing at the cost of a particular pain, except the feelings and judgment of the experienced? When, therefore, those feelings and judgment declare the pleasures derived from the higher faculties to be preferable *in kind,* apart from the question of intensity, to those of which the animal nature, disjoined from the higher faculties, is susceptible, they are entitled on this subject to the same regard.

I have dwelt on this point, as being a necessary part of a perfectly just conception of Utility or Happiness, considered as the directive rule of human conduct. But it is by no means an indispensable condition to the acceptance of the utilitarian standard; for that standard is not the agent's own greatest happiness, but the greatest amount of happiness altogether; and if it may possibly be doubted whether a noble character is always the happier for its nobleness, there can be no doubt that it makes other people happier, and that the world in general is immensely a gainer by it. Utilitarianism, therefore, could only attain its end by the general cultivation of nobleness of character, even if each individual were only benefitted by the nobleness of others, and his own, so far as happiness is concerned, were a sheer deduction from the benefit. But the bare enunciation of such an absurdity as this last, renders refutation superfluous.

According to the Greatest Happiness Principle, as above explained, the ultimate end, with reference to and for the sake of which all other things are desirable (whether we are considering our own good or that of other people), is an existence exempt as far as possible from pain, and as rich as possible in enjoyments, both in point of quantity and quality; the test of quality, and the rule for measuring it against quantity, being the preference felt by those who, in their opportunities of experience, to which must be added their habits of self-consciousness and self-observation, are best furnished with the means of comparison. This, being, according to the utilitarian opinion, the end of human action, is necessarily also the standard of morality; which may accordingly be defined, the rules and precepts for human conduct, by the observance of which an existence such as has been described might be, to the greatest extent possible, secured to all mankind; and not to them only, but, so far as the nature of things admits, to the whole sentient creation.[3]

Against this doctrine, however, arises another class of objectors, who say that happiness, in any form, cannot be the rational purpose of human life and action; because, in the first place, it is unattainable: and they contemptuously ask, What right hast thou to be happy? a question which Mr. Carlyle[4] clenches by the addition, What right, a short time ago, hadst thou even *to be?* Next, they say, that men can do *without* happiness; that all noble human beings have felt this, and could not have become noble but by learning the lesson of Entsagen,[5] or renunciation; which lesson, thoroughly learnt and

9

The rule of human conduct for Mill is the concept of Utility, or

_____.

Underline the clause that begins ''But the greatest amount . . .'' Mill's hedonism is clearly a *social* hedonism.

Mill says that one person's own happiness or pleasure is not adequate as the standard for right and wrong because _____

_____.

10

Read this paragraph slowly. Then reread it. It is a summary of Mill's argument so far.

11

Circle the word *because. Because* often signals that a reason for something is about to be given.

What are the two reasons given by Mill's opponent that happiness cannot be the ''rational purpose of human life and action.''

The first reason is _____.

The second reason is _____ .

What does Mill mean by *happiness* here? _____ .

Why is this sort of happiness impossible? _____ .

Underline the last sentence in this paragraph. Do you think that Mill is optimistic or pessimistic about human happiness?

Mill is _____ about human happiness.

The two ''constituents of a satisfied life'' are (1) _____ and (2) _____ _____ .

submitted to, they affirm to be the beginning and necessary condition of all virtue.

The first of these objections would go to the root of the matter   12 were it well founded; for if no happiness is to be had at all by human beings, the attainment of it cannot be the end of morality, or of any rational conduct. Though, even in that case, something might still be said for the utilitarian theory; since utility includes not solely the pursuit of happiness, but the prevention or mitigation of unhappiness; and if the former aim be chimerical, there will be all the greater scope and more imperative need for the latter, so long at least as mankind think fit to live, and do not take refuge in the simultaneous act of suicide recommended under certain conditions by Novalis.[6] When, however, it is thus positively asserted to be impossible that human life should be happy, the assertion, if not something like a verbal quibble, is at least an exaggeration. If by happiness be meant a continuity of highly pleasurable excitement, it is evident enough that this is impossible. A state of exalted pleasure lasts only moments, or in some cases, and with some intermissions, hours or days, and is the occasional brilliant flash of enjoyment, not its permanent and steady flame. Of this the philosophers who have taught that happiness is the end of life were as fully aware as those who taunt them. The happiness which they meant was not a life of rapture; but moments of such, in an existence made up of few and transitory pains, many and various pleasures, with a decided predominance of the active over the passive, and having as the foundation of the whole, not to expect more from life than it is capable of bestowing. A life thus composed, to those who have been fortunate enough to obtain it, has always appeared worthy of the name of happiness. And such an existence is even now the lot of many, during some considerable portion of their lives. The present wretched education, and wretched social arrangements, are the only real hindrance to its being attainable by almost all.

The objectors perhaps may doubt whether human beings, if   13 taught to consider happiness as the end of life, would be satisfied with such a moderate share of it. But great numbers of mankind have been satisfied with much less. The main constituents of a satisfied life appear to be two, either of which by itself is often found sufficient for the purpose: tranquillity, and excitement. With much tranquillity, many find that they can be content with very little pleasure: with much excitement, many can reconcile themselves to a considerable quantity of pain. There is assuredly no inherent impossibility in enabling even the mass of mankind to unite both; since the two are so far from being incompatible that they are in natural alliance, the prolongation of either being a preparation for, and exciting a wish for, the other. It is only those in whom indolence amounts to a vice, that do not desire excitement after an interval of repose; it is only those in whom the need of excitement is a disease, that feel the tranquillity which follows excitement dull and insipid, instead of pleasurable in direct proportion to the excitement which preceded it. When people who are tolerably fortunate in their outward lot do not find in life sufficient enjoyment to make it valuable to them, the cause generally is, caring for nobody but themselves. To those who have neither public nor private affections, the excitements of life are much curtailed, and in any case dwindle in value as the time approaches when all selfish interests must be terminated by death: while those who leave after them objects of personal affection, and especially those who have also cultivated a fellow-feeling with the collective interests of mankind, retain as lively an interest in life on the eve of death as in the vigour of youth and health. Next to selfishness, the principal cause which makes life unsatisfactory, is want of mental cultivation. A cultivated mind— I do not mean that of a philosopher, but any mind to which the foundations of knowledge have been opened, and which has been taught, in any tolerable degree, to exercise its faculties—finds sources of inexhaustible interest in all that surrounds it; in the objects of nature, the achievements of art, the imaginations of poetry, the incidents of history, the ways of mankind past and present, and their prospects in the future. It is possible, indeed, to become indifferent to all this, and that too without having exhausted a thousandth part of it; but only when one has had from the beginning no moral or human interest in these things, and has sought in them only the gratification of curiosity.

> The two major causes that make life unsatisfactory are (1) _____ _____ and (2) _____ _____ .
>
> Do you think you have a "cultivated mind" in the way Mill describes it? _____ .

Now there is absolutely no reason in the nature of things why an amount of mental culture sufficient to give an intelligent interest in these objects of contemplation, should not be the inheritance of everyone born in a civilized country. As little is there an inherent necessity that any human being should be a selfish egotist, devoid of every feeling or care but those which enter in his own miserable individuality. Something far superior to this is sufficiently common even now, to give ample earnest of what the human species may be made. Genuine private affections, and a sincere interest in the public good, are possible, though in unequal degrees, to every rightly brought up human being. In a world in which there is so much to interest, so much to enjoy, and so much also to correct and improve, everyone who has this moderate amount of moral and intellectual requisites is capable of an existence which may be called enviable; and unless such a person, through bad laws, or subjection to the will of others, is denied the liberty to use the sources of happiness within his reach, he will not fail to find this enviable existence, if he escape the positive evils of life, the great sources of physical and mental suffering—such as indigence, disease, and the unkindness, worthlessness, or premature loss of objects of

> 14

Do you think that Mill is optimistic
or pessimistic about society? I

think Mill is _____
about society.

Underline the sentence beginning
''All the grand sources. . . .'' This
shows whether Mill is an optimist
or pessimist about social problems.

affection. The main stress of the problem lies, therefore, in the contest with these calamities, from which it is a rare good fortune
entirely to escape; which, as things now are, cannot be obviated,
and often cannot be in any material degree mitigated. Yet no one
whose opinion deserves a moment's consideration can doubt that
most of the great positive evils of the world are in themselves
removable, and will, if human affairs continue to improve, be
in the end reduced within narrow limits. Poverty, in any sense
implying suffering, may be completely extinguished by the wisdom
of society, combined with the good sense and providence of
individuals. Even that most intractable of enemies, disease, may be
indefinitely reduced in dimensions by good physical and moral
education, and proper control of noxious influences; while the progress of science holds out a promise for the future of still more direct
conquests over this detestable foe. And every advance in that direction relieves us from some, not only of the chances which cut short
our own lives, but, what concerns us still more, which deprive us
of those in whom our happiness is wrapt up. As for vicissitudes
of fortune, and other disappointments connected with worldly
circumstances, these are principally the effect either of gross impru-
dence, of ill-regulated desires, or of bad or imperfect social institutions.
All the grand sources, in short, of human suffering are in a great
degree, many of them almost entirely, conquerable by human care
and effort; and though their removal is grievously slow—though a
long succession of generations will perish in the breach before the
conquest is completed, and this world becomes all that, if will and
knowledge were not wanting, it might easily be made—yet every
mind sufficiently intelligent and generous to bear a part, however
small and unconspicuous, in the endeavour, will draw a noble
enjoyment from the contest itself, which he would not for any bribe
in the form of selfish indulgence consent to be without.

And this leads to the true estimation of what is said by the   15
objectors concerning the possibility, and the obligation, of learning
to do without happiness. Unquestionably it is possible to do without
happiness; it is done involuntarily by nineteen-twentieths of
mankind, even in those parts of our present world which are least
deep in barbarism; and it often has to be done voluntarily by the
hero or the martyr, for the sake of something which he prizes more
than his individual happiness. But this something, what is it, unless
the happiness of others, or some of the requisites of happiness? It
is noble to be capable of resigning entirely one's own portion of
happiness, or chances of it: but, after all, this self-sacrifice must be
for some end; it is not its own end; and if we are told that its
end is not happiness, but virtue, which is better than happiness,
I ask, would the sacrifice be made if the hero or martyr did not
believe that it would earn for others immunity from similar sacrifices?

Would it be made, if he thought that his renunciation of happiness for himself would produce no fruit for any of his fellow creatures, but to make their lot like his, and place them also in the condition of persons who have renounced happiness? All honour to those who can abnegate for themselves the personal enjoyment of life, when by such renunciation they contribute worthily to increase the amount of happiness in the world; but he who does it, or professes to do it, for any other purpose, is no more deserving of admiration than the ascetic mounted on his pillar. He may be an inspiriting proof of what men *can* do, but assuredly not an example of what they *should*.

For Mill, the "end" of the hero's or the martyr's self-sacrifice is

_____.

Mill has continued to list objections to his ideas. And he has continued to reply to them or refute them. One criticism of utilitarianism that you remember is _____

_____ .

Mill responds to this criticism by saying _____

_____ .

Often philosophical thinking moves in a point, counterpoint, point fashion. That is, an assertion is made, objections are raised, and a response is made to the objections. Not only is this the movement of philosophical thinking, but also it is the movement of much of our thinking much of the time. Remember an incident from your life where the point, counterpoint, point model of thinking was used. Since parents and children use this model all the time, I will use this as an example. One point I originally made was when I said to my parents "I want another cookie." The objection to that point was when my parents said to me "But you have already eaten nine cookies. You will get sick." The response to the objection was when I said "That is OK. I really like cookies and I never get sick." Now you try it.

The point made originally was when I said to my parents

_____

_____ .

The objection to that point was when my parents said _____

_____

_____ .

The response to the objection was when I said _____

_____

_____ .

If you understand the rhythm of this example, then you understand the rhythm of Mill's thought.

The highest virtue found in

humanity is _____ .

Though it is only in a very imperfect state of the world's arrangements that anyone can best serve the happiness of others by the absolute sacrifice of his own, yet so long as the world is in that imperfect state, I fully acknowledge that the readiness to make such a sacrifice is the highest virtue which can be found in man. I will add, that in this condition of the world, paradoxical as the assertion may be, the conscious ability to do without happiness gives the best prospect of realizing such happiness as is attainable. For nothing except that consciousness can raise a person above the chances of life, by making him feel that, let fate and fortune do their worst, they have not power to subdue him: which, once felt, frees him from excess of anxiety concerning the evils of life, and enables him, like many a Stoic in the worst times of the Roman Empire, to cultivate in tranquillity the sources of satisfaction accessible to him, without concerning himself about the uncertainty of their duration, any more than about their inevitable end. 16

Meanwhile, let utilitarians never cease to claim the morality of self-devotion as a possession which belongs by as good a right to them, as either to the Stoic or to the Transcendentalist.[7] The utilitarian morality does recognise in human beings the power of sacrificing their own greatest good for the good of others. It only refuses to admit that the sacrifice is itself a good. A sacrifice which does not increase, or tend to increase, the sum total of happiness, it considers as wasted. The only self-renunciation which it applauds, is devotion to the happiness, or to some of the means of happiness, of others; either of mankind collectively, or of individuals within the limits imposed by the collective interests of mankind. 17

For Mill, a sacrifice is wasted when

_____ .

Name two people you know who have made a sacrifice for something or someone else.

One person I remember is _____ .

Another is _____ .

Was that self-sacrifice something good? _____ . Who might consider that action a good action? _____

_____ . Did that self-sacrifice create a greater good for a greater number of people? _____ . You know the answer to that question and are able to respond because ____

_____

_____

_____

_____.

I must again repeat, what the assailants of utilitarianism seldom have the justice to acknowledge, that the happiness which forms the utilitarian standard of what is right in conduct, is not the agent's own happiness, but that of all concerned. As between his own happiness and that of others, utilitarianism requires him to be as strictly impartial as a disinterested and benevolent spectator. In the golden rule of Jesus of Nazareth, we read the complete spirit of the ethics of utility. To do as one would be done by, and to love one's neighbour as oneself, constitute the ideal perfection of utilitarian morality. As the means of making the nearest approach to this ideal, utility would enjoin, first, that laws and social arrangements should place the happiness, or (as speaking practically it may be called) the interest, of every individual, as nearly as possible in harmony with the interest of the whole; and secondly, that education and opinion, which have so vast a power over human character, should so use that power as to establish in the mind of every individual an indissoluble association between his own happiness and the good of the whole; especially between his own happiness and the practice of such modes of conduct, negative and positive, as regard for the universal happiness prescribes: so that not only he may be unable to conceive the possibility of happiness to himself, consistently with conduct opposed to the general good, but also that a direct impulse to promote the general good may be in every individual one of the habitual motives of action, and the sentiments connected therewith may fill a large and prominent place in every human being's sentient existence. If the impugners of the utilitarian morality represented it to their own minds in this its true character, I know not what recommendation possessed by any other morality they could possibly affirm to be wanting to it: what more beautiful or more exalted developments of human nature any other ethical system can be supposed to foster, or what springs of action, not accessible to the utilitarian, such systems rely on for giving effect to their mandates.

The objectors to utilitarianism cannot always be charged with representing it in a discreditable light. On the contrary, those among them who entertain anything like a just idea of its disinterested character, sometimes find fault with its standard as being too high for humanity. They say it is exacting too much to require that people shall always act from the inducement of promoting the

18

"The requirement" for utilitarianism is _____.

The one word that describes your reaction to this requirement is

_____.

"Education and opinion" should create a link between _____ and _____.

19

Another objection to utilitarianism is that the standard is _____ _____.

general interests of society. But this is to mistake the very meaning of a standard of morals, and to confound the rule of action with the motive of it. It is the business of ethics to tell us what are our duties, or by what test we may know them; but no system of ethics requires that the sole motive of all we do shall be a feeling of duty; on the contrary, ninety-nine hundredths of all our actions are done from other motives, and rightly so done, if the rule of duty does not condemn them. It is the more unjust to utilitarianism that this particular misapprehension should be made a ground of objection to it, inasmuch as utilitarian moralists have gone beyond almost all others in affirming that the motive has nothing to do with the morality of the action, though much with the worth of the agent. He who saves a fellow creature from drowning does what is morally right, whether his motive be duty, or the hope of being paid for his trouble: he who betrays the friend that trusts him, is guilty of a crime, even if his object be to serve another friend to whom he is under greater obligations.* But to speak only of actions done from the motive of duty, and in direct obedience to principle: it is a misapprehension of the utilitarian mode of thought, to conceive it as implying that people should fix their minds upon so wide a generality as the world, or society at large. The great majority of good actions are intended, not for the benefit of the world, but for that of individuals, of which the good of the world is made up; and the thoughts of the most virtuous man need not on these occasions travel beyond the particular persons concerned, except so far as is necessary to assure himself that in benefiting them he is not violating the rights—that is, the legitimate and authorized expectations—of anyone else. The multiplication of happiness is, according to the utilitarian ethics, the object of virtue: the occasions on which any person (except one in a thousand) has it in his power to do this on an extended scale, in other words, to be a public benefactor, are but exceptional; and on these occasions alone is he called on to consider public utility; in every other case, private utility, the interest or happiness of some

Even though much good behavior is intended for the individual or a small circle, this doesn't bother Mill

because _____ .

---

*An opponent, whose intellectual and moral fairness it is a pleasure to acknowledge (the Rev. J. Llewellyn Davies), has objected to this passage, saying, ''Surely the rightness or wrongness of saving a man from drowning does depend very much upon the motive with which it is done. Suppose that a tyrant, when his enemy jumped into the sea to escape from him, saved him from drowning simply in order that he might inflict upon him more exquisite tortures, would it tend to clearness to speak of that rescue as 'a morally right action?' Or suppose again, according to one of the stock illustrations of ethical inquiries, that a man betrayed a trust received from a friend, because the discharge of it would fatally injure that friend himself or someone belonging to him, would utilitarianism compel one to call the betrayal 'a crime' as much as if it had been done from the meanest motive?''

I submit, that he who saves another from drowning in order to kill him by torture afterwards, does not differ only in motive from him who does the same thing from few persons, is all he has to attend to. Those alone the influence of whose actions extends to society in general, need concern themselves habitually about so large an object. In the case of abstinences indeed—of things which people forbear to do, from moral considerations, though the consequences in the particular case might be beneficial—it would be unworthy of an intelligent agent not to be consciously aware that the action is of a class which, if practised generally, would be generally injurious, and that this is the ground of the obligation to abstain from it. The amount of regard for the public interest implied in this recognition, is no greater than is demanded by every system of morals; for they all enjoin to abstain from whatever is manifestly pernicious to society.

The same considerations dispose of another reproach against the doctrine of utility, founded on a still grosser misconception of the purpose of a standard of morality, and of the very meaning of the words right and wrong. It is often affirmed that utilitarianism renders men cold and unsympathizing; that it chills their moral feelings towards individuals; that it makes them regard only the dry and hard consideration of the consequences of actions, not taking into their moral estimate the qualities from which those actions emanate. If the assertion means that they do not allow their judgment respecting the rightness or wrongness of an action to be influenced by their opinion of the qualities of the person who does it, this is a complaint not against utilitarianism, but against having any standard of morality at all; for certainly no known ethical standard decides an action to be good or bad because it is done by a good or a bad man, still less because done by an amiable, a brave, or a benevolent man, or the contrary. These considerations are relevant, not to the estimation of actions, but of persons; and there is nothing in the utilitarian theory inconsistent with the fact that there are other things which interest us in persons besides the rightness and wrongness of their actions. The Stoics, indeed, with the paradoxical misuse of language which was part of their system, and by which

20

The criticism of utilitarianism here is that it makes people _____ _____ and _____ and that it _____ _____ .

---

duty or benevolence; the act itself is different. The rescue of the man is, in the case supposed, only the necessary first step of an act far more atrocious than leaving him to drown would have been. Had Mr. Davies said, ''The rightness or wrongness of saving a man from drowning does depend very much''—not upon the motive, but—''upon the *intention*,'' no utilitarian would have differed from him. Mr. Davies, by an oversight too common not to be quite venial, has in this case confounded the very different ideas of Motive and Intention. There is no point which utilitarian thinkers (and Bentham preeminently) have taken more pains to illustrate than this. The morality of the action depends entirely upon the intention—that is, upon what the agent *wills to do*. But the motive, that is, the feeling which makes him will so to do, when it makes no difference in the act, makes none in the morality: though it makes a great difference in our moral estimation of the agent, especially if it indicates a good or a bad habitual *disposition*—a bent of character from which useful, or from which hurtful actions are likely to arise.

Who does *they* refer to in this sentence?

They refers to _____ .

In this paragraph Mill admits that

there _____
various ways and styles of being utilitarian. [Insert *are* or *are not* in the blank.]

they strove to raise themselves above all concern about anything but virtue, were fond of saying that he who has that has everything; that he, and only he, is rich, is beautiful, is a king. But no claim of this description is made for the virtuous man by the utilitarian doctrine. Utilitarians are quite aware that there are other desirable possessions and qualities besides virtue, and are perfectly willing to allow to all of them their full worth. They are also aware that a right action does not necessarily indicate a virtuous character, and that actions which are blameable often proceed from qualities entitled to praise. When this is apparent in any particular case, it modifies their estimation, not certainly of the act, but of the agent. I grant that they are, notwithstanding of opinion, that in the long run the best proof of a good character is good actions; and resolutely refuse to consider any mental disposition as good, of which the predominant tendency is to produce bad conduct. This makes them unpopular with many people; but it is an unpopularity which they must share with everyone who regards the distinction between right and wrong in a serious light; and the reproach is not one which a conscientious utilitarian need be anxious to repel.

If no more be meant by the objection than that many utilitarians 21 look on the morality of actions, as measured by the utilitarian standard, with too exclusive a regard, and do not lay sufficient stress upon the other beauties of character which go towards making a human being loveable or admirable, this may be admitted. Utilitarians who have cultivated their moral feelings, but not their sympathies nor their artistic perceptions, do fall into this mistake; and so do all other moralists under the same conditions. What can be said in excuse for other moralists is equally available for them, namely, that if there is to be any error, it is better that it should be on that side. As a matter of fact, we may affirm that among utilitarians as among adherents of other systems, there is every imaginable degree of rigidity and of laxity in the application of their standard: some are even puritanically rigorous, while others are as indulgent as can possibly be desired by sinner or by sentimentalist. But on the whole, a doctrine which brings prominently forward the interest that mankind have in the repression and prevention of conduct which violates the moral law, is likely to be inferior to no other in turning the sanctions of opinion against such violations. It is true, the question, What does violate the moral law? is one on which those who recognise different standards of morality are likely now and then to differ. But difference of opinion on moral questions was not first introduced into the world by utilitarianism, while that doctrine does supply, if not always an easy, at all events a tangible and intelligible mode of deciding such differences.

It may not be superfluous to notice a few more of the common 22 misapprehensions of utilitarian ethics, even those which are so obvious and gross that it might appear impossible for any person of candor and intelligence to fall into them: since persons, even of considerable mental endowments, often give themselves so little trouble to understand the bearings of any opinion against which they entertain a prejudice, and men are in general so little conscious of this voluntary ignorance as a defect, that the vulgarest misunderstandings of ethical doctrines are continually met with in the deliberate writings of persons of the greatest pretensions both to high principle and to philosophy. We not uncommonly hear the doctrine of utility inveighed against as a *godless* doctrine. If it be necessary to say anything at all against so mere an assumption, we may say that the question depends upon what idea we have formed of the moral character of the Deity. If it be a true belief that God desires, above all things, the happiness of his creatures, and that this was his purpose in their creation, utility is not only not a godless doctrine, but more profoundly religious than any other. If it be meant that utilitarianism does not recognise the revealed will of God as the supreme law of morals, I answer, that an utilitarian who believes in the perfect goodness and wisdom of God, necessarily believes that whatever God has thought fit to reveal on the subject of morals, must fulfil the requirements of utility in a supreme degree. But others besides utilitarians have been of opinion that the Christian revelation was intended, and is fitted, to inform the hearts and minds of mankind with a spirit which should enable them to find for themselves what is right, and incline them to do it when found, rather than to tell them, except in a very general way, what it is: and that we need a doctrine of ethics, carefully followed out, to *interpret* to us the will of God. Whether this opinion is correct or not, it is superfluous here to discuss; since whatever aid religion, either natural or revealed, can afford to ethical investigation, is as open to the utilitarian moralist as to any other. He can use it as the testimony of God to the usefulness or hurtfulness of any given course of action, by as good a right as others can use it for the indication of a transcendental law, having no connection with usefulness or with happiness.

Still another criticism of utilitarianism is that it is _____

_____.

Circle the word *not* each time it is used in the sentence beginning "If it be a true belief . . . ." This may help you clarify Mill's ideas.

Does Mill think that religion and ethics are separate and distinct?

_____.

In Mill's way of thinking, can one be ethical without believing in God?

_____.

Mill includes another long list of more objections to utilitarianism and another list of responses. But this is not the end. Are there any objections or responses to utilitarianism that you have thought about that have not been addressed yet?

I think another objection to Mill's ideas is _____

_____

_____.

Mill might respond to my objection by saying _____

_____

_____ .

    Notice that you have to imagine what someone else might think to respond to the previous task. Imagination is always important in philosophy.

    In paragraph 22 Mill raises an issue of religion and/or God.

Do you believe in God? _____ I believe (or don't

believe) in God because _____

_____

_____

_____ .

Who and/or what did you imagine God to be when you read the previous question? When I think of God I imagine _____

_____

_____ .

    Is religion important in your mind as you think about ethics?

_____

_____

_____ .

This criticism of utilitarianism

focuses on _____ in

contrast to _____ .

By *expedient*, it is usually meant

_____ .

Circle the word *But*. Then look for the period that ends this sentence and circle it. This is a long sentence. We will refer to this sentence in the dialogue at the end of the chapter.

Again, Utility is often summarily stigmatized as an immoral doctrine by giving it the name of Expediency, and taking advantage of the popular use of that term to contrast it with Principle. But the Expedient, in the sense in which it is opposed to the Right, generally means that which is expedient for the particular interest of the agent himself; as when a minister sacrifices the interest of his country to keep himself in place. When it means anything better than this, it means that which is expedient for some immediate object, some temporary purpose, but which violates a rule whose observance is expedient in a much higher degree. The Expedient, in this sense, instead of being the same thing with the useful, is a branch of the hurtful. Thus, it would often be expedient, for the purpose of getting over some momentary embarrassment, or attaining some object immediately useful to ourselves or others, to tell a lie. But inasmuch as the cultivation in ourselves of a sensitive feeling on the subject of veracity, is one of the most useful, and the enfeeblement of that feeling one of the most hurtful, things to which our conduct can be instrumental; and inasmuch as any, even 23 unintentional, deviation from truth, does that much towards weakening the trustworthiness of human assertion, which is not only the principal support of all present social well-being, but the insufficiency of which does more than any one thing that can be named to keep back civilization, virtue, everything on which human happiness on the largest scale depends; we feel that the violation, for a present advantage, of a rule of such transcendant expediency, is not expedient, and that he who, for the sake of a convenience to himself or to some other individual, does what depends on him to deprive mankind of the good, and inflict upon them the evil, involved in the greater or less reliance which they can place in each other's word, acts the part of one of their worst enemies. Yet that even this rule, sacred as it is, admits of possible exceptions, is acknowledged by all moralists; the chief of which is when the withholding of some fact (as of information from a malefactor, or of bad news from a person dangerously ill) would preserve someone (especially a person other than oneself) from great and unmerited evil, and when the withholding can only be effected by denial. But in order that the exception may not extend itself beyond the need, and may have the least possible effect in weakening reliance on veracity, it ought to be recognised, and, if possible, its limits defined; and if the principle of utility is good for anything, it must be good for weighing these conflicting utilities against one another, and marking out the region within which one or the other preponderates.

Again, defenders of utility often find themselves called upon to reply to such objections as this—that there is not time, pervious to action, for calculating and weighing the effects of any line of conduct on the general happiness. This is exactly as if anyone were to say that it is impossible to guide our conduct, by Christianity, because there is not time, on every occasion on which anything has to be done, to read through the Old and New Testaments. The answer to the objection is, that there has been ample time, namely, the whole past duration of the human species. During all that time mankind have been learning by experience the tendencies of actions; on which experience all the prudence, as well as all the morality of life, is dependent. People talk as if the commencement of this course of experience had hitherto been put off, and as if, at the moment when some man feels tempted to meddle with the property or life of another, he had to begin considering for the first time whether murder and theft are injurious to human happiness. Even then I do not think that he would find the question very puzzling; but, at all events, the matter is now done to his hand. It is truly a whimsical supposition that if mankind were agreed in considering utility to be the test of morality, they would remain without any agreement as to what *is* useful, and would take no measures for having their notions on the subject taught to the young, and

24

This objection to utilitarianism deals with the lack of time for

calculating _____.

Mill's answer to this objection, the objection that there is no time for calculating the effects of an act on

the general happiness, is _____

_____.

enforced by law and opinion. There is no difficulty in proving any ethical standard whatever to work ill, if we suppose universal idiocy to be conjoined with it; but on any hypothesis short of that, mankind must by this time have acquired positive beliefs as to the effects of some actions on their happiness; and the beliefs which have thus come down are the rules of morality for the multitude, and for the philosopher until he has succeeded in finding better. That philosophers might easily do this, even now, on many subjects; that the received code of ethics is by no means of divine right; and that mankind have still much to learn as to the effects of actions on the general happiness, I admit, or rather, earnestly maintain. The corollaries from the principle of utility, like the precepts of every practical art, admit of indefinite improvement, and, in a progressive state of the human mind, their improvement is perpetually going on. But to consider the rules of morality as improvable, is one thing; to pass over the intermediate generalizations entirely, and endeavour to test each individual action directly by the first principle, is another. It is a strange notion that the acknowledgment of a first principle is inconsistent with the admission of secondary ones. To inform a traveller respecting the place of his ultimate destination, is not to forbid the use of landmarks and direction-posts on the way. The proposition that happiness is the end and aim of morality, does not mean that no road ought to be laid down to that goal, or that persons going thither should not be advised to take one direction rather than another. Men really ought to leave off talking a kind of nonsense on this subject, which they would neither talk nor listen to on other matters of practical concernment. Nobody argues that the art of navigation is not founded on astronomy, because sailors cannot wait to calculate the Nautical Almanack. Being rational creatures, they go to sea with it ready calculated; and all rational creatures go out upon the sea of life with their minds made up on the common questions of right and wrong, as well as on many of the far more difficult questions of wise and foolish. And this, as long as foresight is a human quality, it is to be presumed they will continue to do. Whatever we adopt as the fundamental principle of morality, we require subordinate principles to apply it by: the impossibility of doing without them, being common to all systems, can afford no argument against anyone in particular: but gravely to argue as if no such secondary principles could be had, and as if mankind had remained till now, and always must remain, without drawing any general conclusions from the experience of human life, is as high a pitch, I think, as absurdity has ever reached in philosophical controversy.

The remainder of the stock arguments against utilitarianism 25 mostly consist in laying to its charge the common infirmities of human nature, and the general difficulties which embarrass conscientious persons in shaping their course through life. We are told that an utilitarian will be apt to make his own particular case an exception to moral rules, and, when under temptation, will see an utility in the breach of a rule, greater than he will see in its observance. But is utility the only creed which is able to furnish us with excuses for evil doing, and means of cheating our own conscience? They are afforded in abundance by all doctrines which recognise as a fact in morals the existence of conflicting considerations; which all doctrines do, that have been believed by sane persons. It is not the fault of any creed, but of the complicated nature of human affairs, that rules of conduct cannot be so framed as to require no exceptions, and that hardly any kind of action can safely be laid down as either always obligatory or always condemnable. There is no ethical creed which does not temper the rigidity of its laws, by giving a certain latitude, under the moral responsibility of the agent, for accommodation to peculiarities of circumstances; and under every creed, at the opening thus made, self-deception and dishonest casuistry get in. There exists no moral system under which there do not arise unequivocal cases of conflicting obligation. These are the real difficulties, the knotty points both in the theory of ethics, and in the conscientious guidance of personal conduct. They are overcome practically with greater or with less success according to the intellect and virtue of the individual; but it can hardly be pretended that anyone will be the less qualified for dealing with them, from possessing an ultimate standard to which conflicting rights and duties can be referred. If utility is the ultimate source of moral obligations, utility may be invoked to decide between them when their demands are incompatible. Though the application of the standard may be difficult, it is better than none at all: while in other systems, the moral laws all claiming independent authority, there is no common umpire entitled to interfere between them; their claims to precedence one over another rest on little better than sophistry, and unless determined, as they generally are, by the unacknowledged influence of considerations of utility, afford a free scope for the action of personal desires and partialities. We must remember that only in these cases of conflict between secondary principles is it requisite that first principles should be appealed to. There is no case of moral obligation in which some secondary principle is not involved; and if only one, there can seldom be any real doubt which one it is, in the mind of any person by whom the principle itself is recognised.

This criticism of utilitarianism concerns _____ to moral standards.

The real difficulties in both the theory of ethics and in personal conduct are _____ .

For Mill, the ''common umpire'' to make the calls when there are competing ethical claims is _____ _____ .

The primary principle of Mill's ethics is the principle of _____ _____ .

In this chapter, Mill has described what utilitarianism is by voicing objections and then responding to them. Review your underlinings in the chapter, your marginal notes, and your thoughtful responses to the questions in the middle of your reading. This is a difficult task, but it is important to review and synthesize the material.

After you do this, list at least four of the major objections to utilitarianism. Then pair this list with Mill's response to that objection. I have supplied one example for you.

Objection	Response
1 *Utility is opposed to pleasure.*	1 *Utility is based on pleasure or happiness.*
2 _____.	2 _____.
3 _____.	3 _____.
4 _____.	4 _____.
5 _____.	5 _____.

Now paraphrase, or put in your own words, the principle of utility or the greatest happiness principle (review paragraph 2 again if you need to). The principle of utility is _____

_____

_____

_____.

Once you have done this, you have reviewed and summarized the major points in the chapter.

Now, let's try to apply the idea to contemporary life. Let's suppose that you are deciding whether to cheat on your philosophy test. Will your action be right or wrong? Using Mill's criteria, an action is right if it _____ and wrong if it

_____. Imagine that you are John Stuart Mill. Would he say that you should or should not cheat on the test (circle your response)? Now, this is the most important part. Why do you think Mill would say that? Be sure to remember that you are imagining what Mill's reasons might be at this point.

Mill would say that I _____ cheat on the test because the consequences of that action would be _____

_____.

Now, do you think you should cheat on the test? I think I

_____ cheat on the test because _____

_____.

Compare your response to what you imagined Mill's response would be. Are you a utilitarian at this point? _____.

Before you continue, look again at the long sentence in paragraph 23. The introduction gave you a hint about reading these long passages. We advised you that you should ask who or what is happening and to whom or what it is happening. There are many other ways to decipher difficult passages.

Here is another reading technique that may be helpful from time to time. When you encounter an extremely long and complex sentence, make a slash at every punctuation mark. That is, when you see a comma, a semi-colon, a double hyphen, or parentheses, use your pen or pencil and make a mark through the line. It will look like this ''/'' or perhaps like this ''\.'' Now you have divided up the long complicated sentence into shorter segments. Start at the beginning and after you read each segment of the sentence, try to paraphrase it. Try to put that short segment in your own words. And if possible, do this out loud. Hearing your own words and thoughts can be very helpful. After you have translated the phrase, move on to the next one and do the same thing. Before you move to the next phrase, though, go back to the beginning of the sentence and briefly rehearse your paraphrases for the first sections. Then go on to the next segment. Rehearse from the beginning and then proceed to the next section. If you follow this recursive plan, hopefully you will begin to see the connections between the components of the sentence. If you can paraphrase the sentence and understand how the various pieces hang together, then you are well on your way to understanding the sentence.

Notes

1. Epicurus (342–270 B.C.E.) was a Greek philosopher who developed the moral theory called hedonism, in which the criterion for right and wrong action is pleasure. For Epicurus, both pleasure and absence of pain were important. Further, he believed wisdom is demonstrated by the way people make choices regarding pleasure. By pleasure Epicurus did not mean crass physical pleasures. He was ultimately concerned with peace of mind.

2. Stoicism was a dominant philosophical ''school'' during the Hellenistic and Roman periods. For a Stoic, the greatest damage done to reason and ethics was done by human passions.

Since control of mental attitudes toward the world was really the only thing under human agency, stoicism urged acceptance and/or resignation in the face of an often grim reality.

3. *Sentient* means being aware, conscious, or responsive to sense impressions. Mill here is referring to anything in the world that is aware or conscious of the experience of the world.

4. Thomas Carlyle (1795–1881 C.E.) was a Scottish essayist, historian, and philosopher of culture. He had a ''precarious friendship'' with Mill; while they had a joint concern for society, Mill had some problems with Carlyle's authoritarianism.

5. *Entsagen* is the German verb meaning ''to renounce.''

6. Novalis (1772–1801 C.E.) was a lyric poet and leader of the early German romantic movement. Novalis was opposed to the rationalism and the ideals of the Enlightenment.

7. Transcendentalists were a wide group of individuals, both in America and Europe, who were influenced by Plato, German idealism, and often Unitarian Christianity. Ralph Waldo Emerson is a famous example of a transcendentalist in America. Transcendentalists often held a very optimistic and lofty view of humanity.

Chapter 3
Of the Ultimate Sanction of the Principle of Utility

Every moral standard leads to the question: What is the source of obligation to obey this standard? This is true of any moral standard, not just the principle of utility. This question arises when we are asked to adopt a standard, especially one that is different from the one given by our culture and society. Mill continues by articulating both external and internal standards for the principle of utility. External standards are given and enforced by the culture, society, and/or God. Internal standards are those perceived to reside primarily with the individual or with "conscience" rather than with society.

The question is often asked, and properly so, in regard to any supposed moral standard—What is its sanction? what are the motives to obey it? or more specifically, what is the source of its obligation? whence does it derive its binding force? It is a necessary part of moral philosophy to provide the answer to this question; which, though frequently assuming the shape of an objection to the utilitarian morality, as if it had some special applicability to that above others, really arises in regard to all standards. It arises, in fact, whenever a person is called on to *adopt* a standard, or refer morality to any basis on which he has not been accustomed to rest it. For the customary morality, that which education and opinion have consecrated, is the only one which presents itself to the mind with the

1

What do you understand by the word *sanction?*

A "sanction" is _____

_____ .

The question of sanctions arises

when _____ .

feeling of being *in itself* obligatory; and when a person is asked to believe that this morality *derives* its obligation from some general principle round which custom has not thrown the same halo, the assertion is to him a paradox; the supposed corollaries seem to have a more binding force than the original theorem; the superstructure seems to stand better without, than with, what is represented as its foundation. He says to himself, I feel that I am bound not to rob or murder, betray or deceive; but why am I bound to promote the general happiness? If my own happiness lies in something else, why may I not give that the preference?

If the view adopted by the utilitarian philosophy of the nature of the moral sense be correct, this difficulty will always present itself, until the influences which form moral character have taken the same hold of the principle which they have taken of some of the consequences—until, by the improvement of education, the feeling of unity with our fellow creatures shall be (what it cannot be doubted that Christ intended it to be) as deeply rooted in our character, and to our own consciousness as completely a part of our nature, as the horror of crime is in an ordinarily well-brought up young person. In the meantime, however, the difficulty has no peculiar application to the doctrine of utility, but is inherent in every attempt to analyze morality and reduce it to principles; which, unless the principle is already in men's minds invested with as much sacredness as any of its applications, always seems to divest them of part of their sanctity.

2

The word *difficulty* refers to _____ _____.

In this chapter, Mill is dealing with sanctions—the motives to obey or the source of moral obligations. This always comes up when there is any reflection on ethics. Utilitarianism is not unusual or special in this regard. Mill says "I feel I am bound not to rob or murder, betray or deceive, but why am I bound to promote the general happiness?" Ask yourself these questions. Most people

believe that it is wrong to murder someone because _____

_____

_____

_____.

Most people think it is wrong to rob someone because ___

_____

_____

_____.

In thinking about right and wrong actions, the sanctions that are most powerful and most pressing are _____ _____ _____ .

The principle of utility either has, or there is no reason why it might not have, all the sanctions which belong to any other system of morals. Those sanctions are either external or internal. Of the external sanctions it is not necessary to speak at any length. They are, the hope of favor and the fear of displeasure from our fellow creatures or from the Ruler of the Universe, along with whatever we may have of sympathy or affection for them, or of love and awe of Him, inclining us to do his will independently of selfish consequences. There is evidently no reason why all these motives for observance should not attach themselves to the utilitarian morality, as completely and as powerfully as to any other. Indeed, those of them which refer to our fellow creatures are sure to do so, in proportion to the amount of general intelligence; for whether there be any other ground of moral obligation than the general happiness or not, men do desire happiness; and however imperfect may be their own practice, they desire and commend all conduct in others towards themselves, by which they think their happiness is promoted. With regard to the religious motive, if men believe, as most profess to do, in the goodness of God, those who think that conduciveness to the general happiness is the essence, or even only the criterion, of good, must necessarily believe that it is also that which God approves. The whole force therefore of external reward and punishment, whether physical or moral, and whether proceeding from God or from our fellow men, together with all that the capacities of human nature admit, of disinterested devotion to either, become available to enforce the utilitarian morality, in proportion as that morality is recognised; and the more powerfully, the more the appliances of education and general cultivation are bent to the purpose.

So far as to external sanctions. The internal sanction of duty, whatever our standard of duty may be, is one and the same—a feeling in our own mind; a pain, more or less intense, attendant on violation of duty, which in properly cultivated moral natures rises, in the more serious cases, into shrinking from it as an impossibility. This feeling, when disinterested, and connecting itself with the pure idea of duty, and not with some particular form of it, or with any of the merely accessory circumstances, is the essence of Conscience;

3

The two types of sanctions are

(1) _____ and

(2) _____ .

Two external sanctions mentioned by Mill in this paragraph are

(1) _____

(2) _____ .

4

The essense of "conscience" is ___

_____ .

though in that complex phenomenon as it actually exists, the simple fact is in general all encrusted over with collateral associations, derived from sympathy, from love, and still more from fear; from all the forms of religious feeling; from the recollections of childhood and of all our past life; from self-esteem, desire of the esteem of others, and occasionally even self-abasement. This extreme complication is, I apprehend, the origin of the sort of mystical character which, by a tendency of the human mind of which there are many other examples, is apt to be attributed to the idea of moral obligation, and which leads people to believe that the idea cannot possibly attach itself to any other objects than those which, by a supposed mysterious law, are found in our present experience to excite it. Its binding force, however, consists in the existence of a mass of feeling which must be broken through in order to do what violates our standard of right, and which, if we do nevertheless violate that standard, will probably have to be encountered afterwards in the form of remorse. Whatever theory we have of the nature or origin of conscience, this is what essentially constitutes it.

The ultimate sanction, therefore, of all morality (external motives apart) being a subjective feeling in our own minds, I see nothing embarrassing to those whose standard is utility, in the question, what is the sanction of that particular standard? We may answer, the same as of all other moral standards—the conscientious feelings of mankind. Undoubtedly this sanction has no binding efficacy on those who do not possess the feelings it appeals to; but neither will these persons be more obedient to any other moral principle than to the utilitarian one. On them morality of any kind has no hold but through the external sanctions. Meanwhile the feelings exist, a fact in human nature, the reality of which, and the great power with which they are capable of acting on those in whom they have been duly cultivated, are proved by experience. No reason has ever been shown why they may not be cultivated to as great intensity in connection with the utilitarian, as with any other rule of morals.

5

Underline the sentence beginning "We may answer. . . ." Mill says utility has the same sanctions as all other principles of ethics.

Mill says that the ultimate sanction of utilitarianism and of all ethical

systems is _____ .

When you use the word *conscience* you mean _____

_____ .

When he uses the word *conscience* in paragraph 4 Mill means

_____ .

Based on your reading of this chapter, which is more important and fundamental for Mill, internal or external sanctions?

_____ sanctions are more important.

Reflect on your own experience for a moment. One time, one event when some external sanction affected your behavior was when _____

_____

_____

_____ .

One moment when some internal sanction affected your behavior was when _____

_____

_____

_____ .

Do you think that the primary sanction of morality is in the ''conscientious feeling of mankind''—an internal sanction? _____ Why or why not? _____

_____

_____

_____ .

There is, as I am aware, a disposition to belive that a person who sees in moral obligation a transcendental fact, an objective reality belonging to the province of ''Things in themselves,''[1] is likely to be more obedient to it than one who believes it to be entirely subjective, having its seat in human consciousness only. But whatever a person's opinion may be on this point of Ontology,[2] the force he is really urged by is his own subjective feeling, and is exactly measured by its strength. No one's belief that Duty is an objective reality is stronger than the belief that God is so; yet the belief in God, apart from the expectation of actual reward and punishment, only operates on conduct through, and in proportion to, the subjective religious feeling. The sanction, so far as it is disinterested, is always in the mind itself; and the notion therefore of the transcendental moralists must be, that this sanction will not exist *in* the mind unless it is believed to have its root out of the mind; and that if a person is able to say to himself, This which is restraining me, and which is called my conscience, is only a feeling in my own mind, he may possibly draw the conclusion that when the feeling ceases the obligation ceases, and that if he find the feeling inconvenient, he may disregard it, and endeavour to get rid of it. But is this danger confined to the utilitarian morality? Does the belief that moral obligation has its seat outside the mind make the feeling of it too strong to be got rid of? The fact is so far otherwise, that

6

Whether a moral obligation exists outside the mind is not crucial here. The force of morality comes from how that obligation is sensed

_____ .

all moralists admit and lament the ease with which, in the generality of minds, conscience can be silenced or stifled. The question, Need I obey my conscience? is quite as often put to themselves by persons who never heard of the principle of utility, as by its adherents. Those whose conscientious feelings are so weak as to allow of their asking this question, if they answer it affirmatively, will not do so because they believe in the transcendental theory, but because of the external sanctions.

7

It is not necessary, for the present purpose, to decide whether the feeling of duty is innate or implanted. Assuming it to be innate, it is an open question to what objects it naturally attaches itself; for the philosophic supporters of that theory are now agreed that the intuitive perception is of principles of morality, and not of the details. If there be anything innate in the matter, I see no reason why the feeling which is innate should not be that of regard to the pleasures and pains of others. If there is any principle of morals which is intuitively obligatory, I should say it must be that. If so, the intuitive ethics would coincide with the utilitarian, and there would be no further quarrel between them. Even as it is, the intuitive moralists, though they believe that there are other intuitive moral obligations, do already believe this to be one; for they unanimously hold that a large *portion* of morality turns upon the consideration due to the interests of our fellow creatures. Therefore, if the belief in the transcendental origin of moral obligation gives any additional efficacy to the internal sanction, it appears to me that the utilitarian principle has already the benefit of it.

8

On the other hand, if, as is my own belief, the moral feelings are not innate, but acquired, they are not for that reason the less natural. It is natural to man to speak, to reason, to build cities, to cultivate the ground, though these are acquired faculties. The moral feelings are not indeed a part of our nature, in the sense of being in any perceptible degree present in all of us; but this, unhappily, is a fact admitted by those who believe the most strenuously in their transcendental origin. Like the other acquired capacities above referred to, the moral faculty, if not a part of our nature, is a natural outgrowth from it; capable, like them, in a certain small degree, of springing up spontaneously; and susceptible of being brought by cultivation to a high degree of development. Unhappily it is also susceptible, by a sufficient use of the external sanctions and of the force of early impressions, of being cultivated in almost any direction: so that there is hardly anything so absurd or so mischievous that it may not, by means of these influences, be made to act on the human mind with all the authority of conscience. To doubt that the same potency might be given by the same means to the principle of utility, even if it had no foundation in human nature, would be flying in the face of all experience.

Innate means _____ _____. *Implanted* means _____ _____.

Mill believes that moral feelings are not _____ but are rather _____.

But moral associations which are wholly of artificial creation, when intellectual culture goes on, yield by degrees to the dissolving force of analysis: and if the feeling of duty, when associated with utility, would appear equally arbitrary; if there were no leading department of our nature, no powerful class of sentiments, with which that association would harmonize, which would make us feel it congenial, and incline us not only to foster it in others (for which we have abundant interested motives), but also to cherish it in ourselves; if there were not, in short, a natural basis of sentiment for utilitarian morality, it might well happen that this association also, even after it had been implanted by education, might be analyzed away.

9

Do you think the feeling of duty is innate in humans or acquired through experience? The feeling of duty is _____ .

I say this because _____

_____

_____ .

But there *is* this basis of powerful natural sentiment; and this it is which, when once the general happiness is recognised as the ethical standard, will constitute the strength of the utilitarian morality. This firm foundation is that of the social feelings of mankind; the desire to be in unity with our fellow creatures, which is already a powerful principle in human nature, and happily one of those which tend to become stronger, even without express inculcation, from the influences of advancing civilization. The social state is at once so natural, so necessary, and so habitual to man, that, except in some unusual circumstances or by an effort of voluntary abstraction, he never conceives himself otherwise than as a member of a body; and this association is riveted more and more, as mankind are further removed from the state of savage independence. Any condition, therefore, which is essential to a state of society, becomes more and more an inseparable part of every person's conception of the state of things which he is born into, and which is the destiny of a human being. Now, society between human beings, except in the relation of master and slave, is manifestly impossible on any other footing than that the interests of all are to be consulted. Society between equals can only exist on the understanding that the interests of all are to be regarded equally. And since in all states of civilization, every person, except an absolute monarch, has equals, everyone is obliged to live on these terms

10

"This firm foundation" refers to

_____ .

Here Mill is saying that humans

desire _____ with other humans. Putting this in your own

words, you might say _____

_____ .

The _____ relationship is here an exception to Mill's principle.

with somebody; and in every age some advance is made towards a state in which it will be impossible to live permanently on other terms with anybody. In this way people grow up unable to conceive as possible to them a state of total disregard of other people's interests. They are under a necessity of conceiving themselves as at least abstaining from all the grosser injuries, and (if only for their own protection) living in a state of constant protest against them. They are also familiar with the fact of cooperating with others, and proposing to themselves a collective, not an individual, interest, as the aim (at least for the time being) of their actions. So long as they are cooperating, their ends are identified with those of others; there is at least a temporary feeling that the interests of others are their own interests. Not only does all strengthening of social ties, and all healthy growth of society, give to each individual a stronger personal interest in practically consulting the welfare of others; it also leads him to identify his *feelings* more and more with their good, or at least with an ever greater degree of practical consideration for it. He comes, as though instinctively, to be conscious of himself as a being who *of course* pays regard to others. The good of others becomes to him a thing naturally and necessarily to be attended to, like any of the physical conditions of our existence. Now, whatever amount of this feeling a person has, he is urged by the strongest motives both of interest and of sympathy to demonstrate it, and to the utmost of his power encourage it in others; and even if he has none of it himself, he is as greatly interested as anyone else that others should have it. Consequently, the smallest germs of the feeling are laid hold of and nourished by the contagion of sympathy and the influences of education; and a complete web of corroborative association is woven round it, by the powerful agency of the external sanctions. This mode of conceiving ourselves and human life, as civilization goes on, is felt to be more and more natural. Every step in political improvement renders it more so, by removing the sources of opposition of interest, and levelling those inequalities of legal privilege between individuals or classes, owing to which there are large portions of mankind whose happiness it is still practicable to disregard. In an improving state of the human mind, the influences are constantly on the increase, which tend to generate in each individual a feeling of unity with all the rest; which feeling, if perfect, would make him never think of, or desire, any beneficial condition for himself, in the benefits of which they are not included. If we now suppose this feeling of unity to be taught as a religion, and the whole force of education, of institutions, and of opinion, directed, as it once was in the case of religion, to make every person grow up from infancy surrounded on all sides both by the profession and by the practice of it, I think that no one, who can realize this conception, will feel any misgiving about the sufficiency of the ultimate sanction for the Happiness morality. To any ethical student who finds the realization difficult, I recommend, as a means of facilitating it, the second of M. Comte's[3] two principal works, the *Système de Politique Positive.*[*][4] I entertain the strongest objections to the system of politics and morals set forth in that treatise; but I think it has superabundantly shown the possibility of giving to the service of humanity, even without the aid of belief in a Providence, both the psychical power and the social efficacy of a religion; making it take hold of human life, and color all thought, feeling, and action, in a manner of which the greatest ascendancy ever exercised by any religion may be but a type and foretaste; and of which the danger is, not that it should be insufficient, but that it should be so excessive as to interfere unduly with human freedom and individuality.

A good title for this paragraph would be _____ .

11

Neither is it necessary to the feeling which constitutes the binding force of the utilitarian morality on those who recognise it, to wait for those social influences which would make its obligation felt by mankind at large. In the comparatively early state of human advancement in which we now live, a person cannot indeed feel that entireness of sympathy with all others, which would make any real discordance in the general direction of their conduct in life impossible; but already a person in whom the social feeling is at all developed, cannot bring himself to think of the rest of his fellow creatures as struggling rivals with him for the means of happiness, whom he must desire to see defeated in their object in order that he may succeed in his. The deeply rooted conception which every individual even now has of himself as a social being, tends to make him feel it one of his natural wants that there should be harmony between his feelings and aims and those of his fellow creatures. If differences of opinion and of mental culture make it impossible for him to share many of their actual feelings—perhaps make him denounce and defy those feelings—he still needs to be conscious that his real aim and theirs do not conflict; that he is not opposing himself to what they really wish for, namely, their own good, but is, on the contrary, promoting it. This feeling in most individuals is much inferior in strength to their selfish feelings, and is often wanting altogether. But to those who have it, it possesses all the characters of a natural feeling. It does not present itself to their minds as a superstition of education, or a law despotically imposed by the power of society, but as an attribute which it would not be well for them to be without. This conviction is the ultimate sanction of the greatest-happiness morality. This it is which makes any mind, of

The "deeply rooted conception" shared by everyone is _____ _____ .

"This conviction" refers to _____ _____ .

[*Système de politique positive, ou Traité de sociologie, instituant la Religion de l'humanité. 4 vols. Paris: Mathias, 1851–54.]

well-developed feelings, work with, and not against, the outward motives to care for others, afforded by what I have called the external sanctions; and when those sanctions are wanting, or act in an opposite direction, constitutes in itself a powerful internal binding force, in proportion to the sensitiveness and thoughtfulness of the character; since few but those whose mind is a moral blank, could bear to lay out their course of life on the plan of paying no regard to others except so far as their own private interest compels.

Mill has argued that the internal sanction of conscience is more binding and powerful than any other sanction. Mill further states that there is a ''desire to be in unity with our fellow creatures,'' a sympathy with others, a fundamental notion that humans are social and desire harmony between all people.

Do you think Mill is right? Mill's idea is _____. (Insert either *right* or *wrong* in the blank.) List at least three reasons

to support your claim. The first reason Mill is _____

(fill in either *right* or *wrong* from the space above) is _____

_____.

The second reason Mill is _____ is _____

_____.

The third reason Mill is _____ is _____

_____.

Often, humans can dehumanize others around them, make them into animals or demons—the evil ones. List three people or groups who have been considered evil, and thus inhuman, by a good number of the American people. Another way to ask

this is: Who has been the ''enemy''? One enemy has been __

_____. Another enemy has been _____

_____. Another has been _____

_____.

Now list three people or groups you have considered evil, inhuman.

1. _____.

2. _____.

3. _____.

Do your examples create problems for Mill's ideas of a unity between fellow creatures? My examples _____ create problems for Mill's ideas because _____

_____

_____

_____ .

Notes

1. "Things in themselves" is a reference to Kant and the German phrase "Ding an sich."

2. Ontology is the subsection of philosophy concerned with the study of being.

3. Auguste Comte (1798–1857 C.E.) was a French social philosopher. His "positivism" sought a foundation for a new science— sociology—which abandoned the search for external causes of the material world (such as religion and God) in favor of focusing on the correlation of empirical, "positive," facts of observation.

4. *Système de Politique Positive* was the title of Comte's treatise setting out the principles of his Course of Positive Politics.

Chapter 4

Of What Sort of Proof the Principle of Utility Is Susceptible

In this short chapter, Mill returns to an issue raised in the first chapter—that of the issue of proof and utilitarianism. Mill argues that the question of ultimate ends regarding ethics is, really, the question of what is desirable. Furthermore, Mill claims that happiness is the *only* thing desired by humans. What is the proof? For Mill, the proof is that people desire happiness and never desire anything else. Virtue, money, power, fame, and anything else one wanted to list would be merely means to happiness. "Happiness is the sole end of human action, and the promotion of it the test by which to judge of all human conduct. . . ." What about those acts of will that seem not informed by a desire for happiness? Mill asserts that the human will is "the child of desire," and ceases to be under the control of desire when formed into habit. Thus even acts of the will become subordinate to the desire for good. And "if this doctrine be true, the principle of utility is proved."

"The former" refers to

_____ .

It has already been remarked, that questions of ultimate ends   1
do not admit of proof, in the ordinary acceptation of the term. To
be incapable of proof by reasoning is common to all first principles;
to the first premises of our knowledge, as well as to those of our
conduct. But the former, being matters of fact, may be the subject
of a direct appeal to the faculties which judge of fact—namely, our

senses, and our internal consciousness. Can an appeal be made to the same faculties on questions of practical ends? Or by what other faculty is cognizance taken of them?

Questions about ends are, in other words, questions about what things are desirable. The utilitarian doctrine is, that happiness is desirable, and the only thing desirable, as an end; all other things being only desirable as means to that end. What ought to be required of this doctrine—what conditions is it requisite that the doctrine should fulfill—to make good its claim to be believed?

The only proof capable of being given that an object is visible, is that people actually see it. The only proof that a sound is audible, is that people hear it: and so of the other sources of our experience. In like manner, I apprehend, the sole evidence it is possible to produce that anything is desirable, is that people do actually desire it. If the end which the utilitarian doctrine proposes to itself were not, in theory and in practice, acknowledged to be an end, nothing could ever convince any person that it was so. No reason can be given why the general happiness is desirable, except that each person, so far as he believes it to be attainable, desires his own happiness. This, however, being a fact, we have not only all the proof which the case admits of, but all which it is possible to require, that happiness is a good: that each person's happiness is a good to that person, and the general happiness, therefore, a good to the aggregate of all persons. Happiness has made out its title as *one* of the ends of conduct, and consequently one of the criteria of morality.

2

Utilitarianism claims that the **only** desirable end is _____.

3

Underline the only evidence for the assertion that ''anything is desirable.''

''This, . . . being a fact'' refers to

_____.

Mill says that ''the only proof capable of being given that an object is visible is that people see it. The only proof that a sound is audible, is that people hear it. . . .'' Fill in some other similar examples from your experience.

The only proof capable of being given that _____

is that _____.

The only proof capable of being given that _____ is

that _____.

The only proof capable of being given that _____ is

that _____.

''In like manner,'' or by analogy, Mill says that ''the only evidence . . . that anything is desirable, is that people do actually desire it.'' This argument by analogy will be Mill's entrance into proving that happiness is the sole criterion for right and wrong.

Here you should note a possible problem in Mill's thought. Ask yourself this: From the fact that people do desire something, does it actually follow that they ought to do that something? Imagine that someone has a desire to hurt children. That is given, a fact. This person admits publicly that it is his desire to hurt children. Does it follow that this person should hurt children? The fallacy of moving from ''what is'' to ''what ought to be'' is often called the naturalistic fallacy. A criticism of Mill is that he commits this fallacy in *Utilitarianism.*

Opponents of utilitarianism argue that there are other goals of human action beside _____ .

But it has not, by this alone, proved itself to be the sole criterion.   4
To do that, it would seem, by the same rule, necessary to show, not only that people desire happiness, but that they never desire anything else. Now it is palpable that they do desire things which, in common language, are decidedly distinguished from happiness. They desire, for example, virtue, and the absence of vice, no less really than pleasure and the absence of pain. The desire of virtue is not as universal, but it is as authentic a fact, as the desire of happiness. And hence the opponents of the utilitarian standard deem that they have a right to infer that there are other ends of human action besides happiness, and that happiness is not the standard of approbation and disapprobation.

But does the utilitarian doctrine deny that people desire virtue,   5
or maintain that virtue is not a thing to be desired? The very reverse. It maintains not only that virtue is to be desired, but that it is to be desired disinterestedly, for itself. Whatever may be the opinion of utilitarian moralists as to the original conditions by which virtue is made virtue; however they may believe (as they do) that actions and dispositions are only virtuous because they promote another end than virtue; yet this being granted, and it having been decided, from considerations of this description, what *is* virtuous, they not only place virtue at the very head of the things which are good as means to the ultimate end, but they also recognise as a psychological fact the possibility of its being, to the individual, a good in itself, without looking to any end beyond it; and hold, that the mind is not in a right state, not in a state conformable to Utility, not in the state most conducive to the general happiness, unless it does love virtue in this manner—as a thing desirable in itself, even although, in the individual instance, it should not produce those other desirable consequences which it tends to produce, and on account of which it is held to be virtue. This opinion is not, in the smallest degree, a departure from the Happiness principle. The ingredients of happiness are very various, and each of them is desirable in itself, and not merely when considered as swelling an aggregate. The principle of utility does not mean that any given pleasure, as music, for instance, or any given exemption from pain, as for example health, are to be looked upon as means to a collective something termed

Circle the word *whatever.* Then look for the period that ends the sentence and circle it. Again, this is a long sentence. We will refer to it in the next dialogue.

happiness, and to be desired on that account. They are desired and desirable in and for themselves; besides being means, they are a part of the end. Virtue, according to the utilitarian doctrine, is not naturally and originally part of the end, but it is capable of becoming so; and in those who love it disinterestedly it has become so, and is desired and cherished, not as a means to happiness, but as a part of their happiness.

To illustrate this farther, we may remember that virtue is not the only thing, originally a means, and which if it were not a means to anything else, would be and remain indifferent, but which by association with what it is a means to, comes to be desired for itself, and that too with the utmost intensity. What, for example, shall we say of the love of money? There is nothing originally more desirable about money than about any heap of glittering pebbles. Its worth is solely that of the things which it will buy; the desires for other things than itself, which it is a means of gratifying. Yet the love of money is not only one of the strongest moving forces of human life, but money is, in many cases, desired in and for itself; the desire to possess it is often stronger than the desire to use it, and goes on increasing when all the desires which point to ends beyond it, to be compassed by it, are failing off. It may be then said truly, that money is desired not for the sake of an end, but as part of the end. From being a means to happiness, it has come to be itself a principal ingredient of the individual's conception of happiness. The same may be said of the majority of the great objects of human life—power, for example, or fame; except that to each of these there is a certain amount of immediate pleasure annexed, which has at least the semblance of being naturally inherent in them; a thing which cannot be said of money. Still, however, the strongest natural attraction, both of power and of fame, is the immense aid they give to the attainment of our other wishes; and it is the strong association thus generated between them and all our objects of desire, which gives to the direct desire of them the intensity it often assumes, so as in some characters to surpass in strength all other desires. In these cases the means have become a part of the end, and a more important part of it than any of the things which they are means to. What was once desired as an instrument for the attainment of happiness, has come to be desired for its own sake. In being desired for its own sake it is, however, desired as *part* of happiness. The person is made, or thinks he would be made, happy by its mere possession; and is made unhappy by failure to obtain it. The desire of it is not a different thing from the desire of happiness, any more than the love of music, or the desire of health. They are included in happiness. They are some of the elements of which the desire of happiness is made up. Happiness is not an abstract idea, but a concrete whole; and these are some of its parts. And

What is the difference between a "means" and an "end"?

A means is _____ ,

while an end is _____ .

6

The example or illustration that

Mill uses here is _____

_____ .

Two other examples used by Mill

are _____ and

_____ .

the utilitarian standard sanctions and approves their being so. Life would be a poor thing, very ill provided with sources of happiness, if there were not this provision of nature, by which things originally indifferent, but conducive to, or otherwise associated with, the satisfaction of our primitive desires, become in themselves sources of pleasure more valuable than the primitive pleasures, both in permanency, in the space of human existence that they are capable of covering, and even in intensity.

Virtue, according to the utilitarian conception, is a good of this description. There was no original desire of it, or motive to it, save its conduciveness to pleasure, and especially to protection from pain. But through the association thus formed, it may be felt a good in itself, and desired as such with as great intensity as any other good; and with this difference between it and the love of money, of power, or of fame, that all of these may, and often do, render the individual noxious to the other members of the society to which he belongs, whereas there is nothing which makes him so much a blessing to them as the cultivation of the disinterested love of virtue. And consequently, the utilitarian standard, while it tolerates and approves those other acquired desires, up to the point beyond which they would be more injurious to the general happiness than promotive of it, enjoins and requires the cultivation of the love of virtue up to the greatest strength possible, as being above all things important to the general happiness. 7

Underline the first two sentences of this paragraph. They are important because Mill restates that happiness is the criterion for determining right and wrong actions.

It results from the preceding considerations, that there is in reality nothing desired except happiness. Whatever is desired otherwise than as a means to some end beyond itself, and ultimately to happiness, is desired as itself a part of happiness, and is not desired for itself until it has become so. Those who desire virtue for its own sake, desire it either because the consciousness of it is a pleasure, or because the consciousness of being without it is a pain, or for both reasons united; as in truth the pleasure and pain seldom exist separately, but almost always together, the same person feeling pleasure in the degree of virtue attained, and pain in not having attained more. If one of these gave him no pleasure, and the other no pain, he would not love or desire virtue, or would desire it only for the other benefits which it might produce to himself or to persons whom he cared for. 8

Mill concludes that humans desire nothing except _____ .

Mill says he has demonstrated that humans do not want anything but happiness; if they desire anything else, it is merely a means to happiness or a part of happiness itself.

Your best friend has become interested in your studies again. Paraphrase or put in your own words for her Mill's ideas demonstrating the part about happiness. Explain it so that your best friend will understand. Humans do not desire anything but

_____. If they say they desire something

else, that is because _____

_____

_____ .

    Look again at the long sentence in paragraph 5.
I was able to understand this sentence by using the technique

of _____

_____

_____ .

We have now, then, an answer to the question, what sort of proof the principle of utility is susceptible. If the opinion which I have now stated is psychologically true—if human nature is so constituted as to desire nothing which is not either a part of happiness or a means of happiness, we can have no other proof, and we require no other, that these are the only things desirable. If so, happiness is the sole end of human action, and the promotion of it the test by which to judge of all human conduct; from whence it necessarily follows that it must be the criterion of morality, since a part is included in the whole.

And now to decide whether this is really so; whether mankind do desire nothing for itself but that which is a pleasure to them, or of which the absence is a pain; we have evidently arrived at a question of fact and experience, dependent, like all similar questions, upon evidence. It can only be determined by practiced self-consciousness and self-observation, assisted by observation of others. I believe that these sources of evidence, impartially consulted, will declare that desiring a thing and finding it pleasant, aversion to it and thinking of it as painful, are phenomena entirely inseparable, or rather two parts of the same phenomenon; in strictness of language, two different modes of naming the same psychological fact: that to think of an object as desirable (unless for the sake of its consequences), and to think of it as pleasant, are one and the same thing; and that to desire anything, except in proportion as the idea of it is pleasant, is a physical and metaphysical impossibility.

So obvious does this appear to me, that I expect it will hardly be disputed: and the objection made will be, not that desire can possibly be directed to anything ultimately except pleasure and exemption from pain, but that the will is a different thing from desire; that a person of confirmed virtue, or any other person whose

9
Read this paragraph slowly. Here Mill states the key idea of this chapter.

Circle "whence it necessarily follows." This phrase usually indicates that a conclusion will follow. What is Mill's conclusion

here? _____ .
What is the reason that he gives for this conclusion? _____ .

10

Evidence for Mill's conclusion comes from three sources:

(1) _____ ; (2) _____

_____ ; and (3) _____ .

11

An objection will be made that

"will" is different from "_____

_____ ."

purposes are fixed, carries out his purposes without any thought of the pleasure he has in contemplating them, or expects to derive from their fulfillment; and persists in acting on them, even though these pleasures are much diminished, by changes in his character or decay of his passive sensibilities, or are outweighed by the pains which the pursuit of the purposes may bring upon him. All this I fully admit, and have stated it elsewhere,[*][1] as positively and emphatically as anyone. Will, the active phenomenon, is a different thing from desire, the state of passive sensibility, and though originally an offshoot from it, may in time take root and detach itself from the parent stock; so much so, that in the case of an habitual purpose, instead of willing the thing because we desire it, we often desire it only because we will it. This, however, is but an instance of that familiar fact, the power of habit, and is nowise confined to the case of virtuous actions. Many indifferent things, which men originally did from a motive of some sort, they continue to do from habit. Sometimes this is done unconsciously, the consciousness coming only after the action: at other times with conscious volition, but volition which has became habitual, and is put into operation by the force of habit, in opposition perhaps to the deliberate preference, as often happens with those who have contracted habits of vicious or hurtful indulgence. Third and last comes the case in which the habitual act of will in the individual instance is not in contradiction to the general intention prevailing at other times, but in fulfillment of it; as in the case of the person of confirmed virtue, and of all who pursue deliberately and consistently any determinate end. The distinction between will and desire thus understood, is an authentic and highly important psychological fact; but the fact consists solely in this—that will, like all other parts of our constitution, is amenable to habit, and that we may will from habit what we no longer desire for itself, or desire only because we will it. It is not the less true that will, in the beginning, is entirely produced by desire; including in that term the repelling influence of pain as well as the attractive one of pleasure. Let us take into consideration, no longer the person who has a confirmed will to do right, but him in whom that virtuous will is still feeble, conquerable by temptation, and not to be fully relied on; by what means can it be strengthened? How can the will to be virtuous, where it does not exist in sufficient force, be implanted or awakened? Only by making the person *desire* virtue—by making him think of it in a pleasurable light, or of its absence in a painful one. It is by associating the doing right with pleasure, or the doing wrong with pain, or by eliciting and impressing and bringing home to the person's

Underline the sentence beginning
''The distinction between . . .''
Here Mill addresses the will/desire distinction.

[*See *A System of Logic*. 8th ed. 2 vols. London: Longmans, Green, Reader, and Dyer, 1872, Vol. II, pp. 428–9 (Book VI, Chap. ii, § 4).]

experience the pleasure naturally involved in the one or the pain in the other, that it is possible to call forth that will to be virtuous, which, when confirmed, acts without any thought of either pleasure or pain. Will is the child of desire, and passes out of the dominion of its parent only to come under that of habit. That which is the result of habit affords no presumption of being intrinsically good; and there would be no reason for wishing that the purpose of virtue should become independent of pleasure and pain, were it not that the influence of the pleasurable and painful associations which prompt to virtue is not sufficiently to be depended on for unerring constancy of action until it has acquired the support of habit. Both in feeling and in conduct, habit is the only thing which imparts certainty; and it is because of the importance to others of being able to rely absolutely on one's feelings and conduct, and to oneself of being able to rely on one's own, that the will to do right ought to be cultivated into this habitual independence. In other words, this state of the will is a means to good, not intrinsically a good; and does not contradict the doctrine that nothing is a good to human beings but in so far as it is either itself pleasurable, or a means of attaining pleasure or averting pain.

But if this doctrine be true, the principle of utility is proved. Whether it is so or not, must now be left to the consideration of the thoughtful reader.

Underline the sentence beginning "Will is the child of desire . . ." Mill continues to address the will/desire distinction.

Underline the last sentence in this paragraph. The will is a _____ to a good, not _____ a good.
12
What would you imagine are three characteristics of "a thoughtful reader"?
One characteristic of a thoughtful reader would be _____ .
Another would be _____ .
Still another characteristic of a thoughtful reader would be _____ _____ .

You are almost finished with your close, careful, and slow reading of a classic text in the history of Western philosophy. Periodically, it is good to review larger "chunks" of material so that the ideas stick together. Thinking back to the beginning of your reading of *Utilitarianism*, Chapter 1, "General Remarks," is about ____

_____

_____ .

Chapter 2, "What Utilitarianism Is," about _____

_____

_____ .

Chapter 3, "Of the Ultimate Sanction of the Principle of Utility," is about _____

_____

_____ .

Chapter 4, "Of What Sort of Proof the Principle of Utility Is Susceptible," is about _____

_____
_____.

So far the main idea that I have distilled from the reading is

_____
_____.

Notes

1. *A System of Logic,* Book VI: A reference to Mill's earlier work
    on logic. See Appendix 2 for more information on this work
    and other writings by Mill.

Chapter 5
On the Connection between Justice and Utility

This long and complicated last chapter responds to the common charge against any ethical theory that focuses on consequences. The charge is that *justice* is an inherent quality or a criterion that is prior or superior to any invocation of the principle of utility. Further, using justice as an ethical criterion is supposed to create clarity and simplicity in the moral life. But after analysis of the way justice is used in ethical theory, Mill is left not with clarity, but with confusion and contradictory views on the nature of justice. Mill's conclusion: Justice itself is based on utility, the greatest happiness principle. ''I account the justice which is grounded on utility to be the chief part, and incomparably the most sacred and binding part, of all morality.'' Thus, for Mill, the ''only real difficulty'' facing utilitarianism has been answered. The issue of ethics is resolved. The criterion for judging right and wrong is in place.

In all ages of speculation, one of the strongest obstacles to the reception of the doctrine that Utility or Happiness is the criterion of right and wrong, has been drawn from the idea of Justice. The powerful sentiment, and apparently clear perception, which that word recalls with a rapidity and certainty resembling an instinct, have seemed to the majority of thinkers to point to an inherent quality in things; to show that the Just must have an existence in Nature as something

1

An obstacle to utilitarianism is the idea that _____ is an _____ quality in things (existence), not the principle of utility.

absolute—generically distinct from every variety of the Expedient, and, in idea, opposed to it, though (as is commonly acknowledged) never, in the long run, disjoined from it in fact.

In the case of this, as of our other moral sentiments, there is no 2 necessary connection between the question of its origin, and that of its binding force. That a feeling is bestowed on us by Nature, does not necessarily legitimate all its promptings. The feeling of justice might be a peculiar instinct, and might yet require, like our other instincts, to be controlled and enlightened by a higher reason. If we have intellectual instincts, leading us to judge in a particular way, as well as animal instincts that prompt us to act in a particular way, there is no necessity that the former should be more infallible in their sphere than the latter in theirs: it may as well happen that wrong judgments are occasionally suggested by those, as wrong actions by these. But though it is one thing to believe that we have natural feelings of justice, and another to acknowledge them as an ultimate criterion of conduct, these two opinions are very closely connected in point of fact. Mankind are always predisposed to believe that any subjective feeling, not otherwise accounted for, is a revelation of some objective reality. Our present object is to determine whether the reality, to which the feeling of justice corresponds, is one which needs any such special revelation; whether the justice or injustice of an action is a thing intrinsically peculiar, and distinct from all its other qualities, or only a combination of certain of those qualities, presented under a peculiar aspect. For the purpose of this inquiry, it is practically important to consider whether the feeling itself, of justice and injustice, is *sui generis*[1] like our sensations of color and taste, or a derivative feeling, formed by a combination of others. And this it is the more essential to examine, as people are in general willing enough to allow, that objectively the dictates of justice coincide with a part of the field of General Expediency; but inasmuch as the subjective mental feeling of Justice is different from that which commonly attaches to simple expediency, and, except in extreme cases of the latter, is far more imperative in its demands, people find it difficult to see, in Justice, only a particular kind or branch of general utility, and think that its superior binding force requires a totally different origin.

To throw light upon this question, it is necessary to attempt 3 to ascertain what is the distinguishing character of justice, or of injustice: what is the quality, or whether there is any quality, attributed in common to all modes of conduct designated as unjust (for justice, like many other moral attributes, is best defined by its opposite), and distinguishing them from such modes of conduct as are disapproved, but without having that particular epithet of disapprobation applied to them. If, in everything which men are accustomed to characterize as just or unjust, some one common attribute

Mill's concern here is to determine if justice is either distinct from

other qualities or _____ .

Restate what "people find . . . difficult to see." Putting it in your

own words, you might say _____

_____ .

This will be the guiding idea of this last chapter.

or collection of attributes is always present, we may judge whether this particular attribute or combination of attributes would be capable of gathering round it a sentiment of that peculiar character and intensity by virtue of the general laws of our emotional constitution, or whether the sentiment is inexplicable, and requires to be regarded as a special provision of Nature. If we find the former to be the case, we shall, in resolving this question, have resolved also the main problem: if the latter, we shall have to seek for some other mode of investigating it.

What would be a good title for this paragraph? Place your title in the margin at the beginning of the paragraph.

So far in this chapter, the issue is justice, and whether it is distinctive or derived from something else. Try to anticipate Mill's line of thinking.

Mill will eventually say that the notion of justice is _____.
You may change your mind as you read, but anticipating often serves to encourage your reading and make it active. You want to find out if you are right or not.
Now, what do *you* think? Is justice derived from something more basic than justice? Or is justice itself basic and fundamental?

I think justice is _____, because _____

_____

_____ .

To anticipate what Mill will discuss next, write down what you think is the distinguishing character of justice.
The common element in everything that I consider just is

_____ .

To find the common attributes of a variety of objects, it is 4 necessary to begin by surveying the objects themselves in the concrete. Let us therefore advert successively to the various modes of action, and arrangements of human affairs, which are classed, by universal or widely spread opinion, as Just or Unjust. The things well known to excite the sentiments associated wtih those names, are of a very multifarious character. I shall pass them rapidly in review, without studying any particular arrangement.

In the first place, it is mostly considered unjust to deprive any- 5 one of his personal liberty, his property, or any other thing which belongs to him by law. Here, therefore, is one instance of the application of the terms just and unjust in a perfectly definite sense, namely, that it is just to respect, unjust to violate, the *legal rights* of anyone. But this judgment admits of several exceptions, arising from the other forms in which the notions of justice and injustice

It seems unjust to _____ .

present themselves. For example, the person who suffers the deprivation may (as the phrase is) have *forfeited* the rights which he is so deprived of: a case to which we shall return presently. But also,

Secondly; the legal rights of which he is deprived, may be rights 6 which *ought* not to have belonged to him; in other words, the law which confers on him these rights, may be a bad law. When it is so, or when (which is the same thing for our purpose) it is supposed to be so, opinions will differ as to the justice or injustice of infringing it. Some maintain that no law, however bad, ought to be disobeyed by an individual citizen; that his opposition to it, if shown at all, should only be shown in endeavoring to get it altered by competent authority. This opinion (which condemns many of the most illustrious benefactors of mankind, and would often protect pernicious institutions against the only weapons which, in the state of things existing at the time, have any chance of succeeding against them) is defended, by those who hold it, on grounds of expediency; principally on that of the importance, to the common interest of mankind, of maintaining inviolate the sentiment of submission to law. Other persons, again, hold the directly contrary opinion, that any law, judged to be bad, may blamelessly be disobeyed, even though it be not judged to be unjust, but only inexpedient; while others would confine the license of disobedience to the case of unjust laws: but again, some say, that all laws which are inexpedient are unjust; since every law imposes some restriction on the natural liberty of mankind, which restriction is an injustice, unless legitmated by tending to their good. Among these diversities of opinion, it seems to be universally admitted that there may be unjust laws, and that law, consequently, is not the ultimate criterion of justice, but may give to one person a benefit or impose on another an evil, which justice condemns. When, however, a law is thought to be unjust, it seems always to be regarded as being so in the same way in which a breach of law is unjust, namely, by infringing somebody's right; which, as it cannot in this case be a legal right, receives a different appellation, and is called a moral right. We may say, therefore, that a second case of injustice consists in taking or withholding from any person that to which he has a *moral right*.

Thirdly, it is universally considered just that each person should 7 obtain that (whether good or evil) which he *deserves*; and unjust that he should obtain a good, or be made to undergo an evil, which he does not deserve. This is, perhaps, the clearest and most emphatic form in which the idea of justice is conceived by the general mind. As it involves the notion of desert, the question arises, what constitutes desert? Speaking in a general way, a person is understood to deserve good if he does right, evil if he does wrong; and in a

Law cannot be the ultimate criterion of justice because

_____ .

The second case of injustice is

_____ .

Something is just when one gets what one _____ .

more particular sense, to deserve good from those to whom he does or has done good, and evil from those to whom he does or has done evil. The precept of returning good for evil has never been regarded as a case of the fulfillment of justice, but as one in which the claims of justice are waived, in obedience to other considerations.

Fourthly, it is confessedly unjust to *break faith* with anyone: to violate an engagement, either express or implied, or disappoint expectations raised by our own conduct, at least if we have raised those expectations knowingly and voluntarily. Like the other obligations of justice already spoken of, this one is not regarded as absolute, but as capable of being overruled by a stronger obligation of justice on the other side; or by such conduct on the part of the person concerned as is deemed to absolve us from our obligation to him, and to constitute a *forfeiture* of the benefit; which he has been led to expect.

8

The injustice described in this paragraph is _____.

Fifthly, it is by universal admission, inconsistent with justice to be *partial*; to show favor or preference to one person over another, in matters to which favor and preference do not properly apply. Impartiality, however, does not seem to be regarded as a duty in itself, but rather as instrumental to some other duty; for it is admitted that favor and preference are not always censurable, and indeed the cases in which they are condemned are rather the exception than the rule. A person would be more likely to be blamed than applauded for giving his family or friends no superiority in good offices over strangers, when he could do so without violating any other duty; and no one thinks it unjust to seek one person in preference to another as a friend, connection, or companion. Impartiality where rights are concerned is of course obligatory, but this is involved in the more general obligation of giving to every one his right. A tribunal, for example, must be impartial, because it is bound to award, without regard to any other consideration, a disputed object to the one of two parties who has the right to it. There are other cases in which impartiality means, being solely influenced by desert; as with those who, in the capacity of judges, preceptors, or parents, administer reward and punishment as such. There are cases, again, in which it means, being solely influenced by consideration for the public interest; as in making a selection among candidates for a government employment. Impartiality, in short, as an obligation of justice, may be said to mean, being exclusively influenced by the considerations which it is supposed ought to influence the particular case in hand; and resisting the solicitation of any motives which prompt to conduct different from what those considerations would dictate.

9

Another injustice appears to be

_____.

Nearly allied to the idea of impartiality, is that of *equality;* which often enters as a component part both into the conception of justice and into the practice of it, and, in the eyes of many persons,

10
Yet another injustice would be

_____.

Underline the sentence beginning "But in this, still . . . ." Here Mill gives you a hint about his conclusion regarding justice. Do you think, now, that Mill will say that justice is a distinctive quality or a derived quality?

For Mill, justice is a _____ quality.

constitutes its essence. But in this, still more than in any other case, the notion of justice varies in different persons, and always conforms in its variations to their notion of utility. Each person maintains that equality is the dictate of justice, except where he thinks that expediency requires inequality. The justice of giving equal protection to the rights of all, is maintained by those who support the most outrageous inequality in the rights themselves. Even in slave countries it is theoretically admitted that the rights of the slave, such as they are, ought to be as sacred as those of the master; and that a tribunal which fails to enforce them with equal strictness is wanting in justice; while, at the same time, institutions which leave to the slave scarcely any rights to enforce, are not deemed unjust, because they are not deemed inexpedient. Those who think that utility requires distinctions of rank, do not consider it unjust that riches and social privileges should be unequally dispensed; but those who think this inequality inexpedient, think it unjust also. Whoever thinks that government is necessary, sees no injustice in as much inequality as is constituted by giving to the magistrate powers not granted to other people. Even among those who hold leveling doctrines, there are as many questions of justice as there are differences of opinion about expediency. Some Communists[2] consider it unjust that the produce of the labor of the community should be shared on any other principle than that of exact equality; others think it just that those should receive most whose needs are greatest; while others hold that those who work harder, or who produce more, or whose services are more valuable to the community, may justly claim a larger quota in the division of the produce. And the sense of natural justice may be plausibly appealed to in behalf of every one of these opinions.

Mill has presented a list of characteristics of justice. Can *you* add other characteristics to that list?

Something is just if _____

_____ .

Something is unjust if _____

_____ .

Among so many diverse applications of the term Justice, which   11 yet is not regarded as ambiguous, it is a matter of some difficulty to seize the mental link which holds them together, and on which the moral sentiment adhering to the term essentially depends. Perhaps, in this embarrassment, some help may be derived from the history of the word, as indicated by its etymology.[3]

"This embarrassment" refers to

_____ .

In most, if not in all, languages, the etymology of the word which
corresponds to Just, points to an origin connected either with
positive law, or with that which was in most cases the primitive form
of law—authoritative custom. *Justum*[4] is a form of *jussum,* that which
has been ordered. *Jus* is of the same origin. Δίκαιον[5] comes from
δίκη,[6] of which the principal meaning, at least in the historical ages
of Greece, was a suit at law. Originally, indeed, it meant only the
mode or *manner* of doing things, but it early came to mean the
prescribed manner; that which the recognised authorities, patriarchal,
judicial, or political, would enforce. *Recht,*[7] from which came *right*
and *righteous,* is synonymous with law. The original meaning indeed
of *recht* did not point to law, but to physical straightness; as *wrong*
and its Latin equivalents meant twisted or *tortuous;* and from this
it is argued that right did not originally mean law, but on the contrary law meant right. But however this may be, the fact that *recht*
and *droit*[8] became restricted in their meaning to positive law,
although much which is not required by law is equally necessary
to moral straightness or rectitude, is as significant of the original
character of moral ideas as if the derivation had been the reverse
way. The courts of justice, the administration of justice, are the
courts and the administration of law. *La justice,* in French, is the
established term for judicature. There can, I think, be no doubt that
the *idée mère,* the primitive element, in the formation of the notion
of justice, was conformity to law. It constituted the entire idea among
the Hebrews, up to the birth of Christianity; as might be expected
in the case of a people whose laws attempted to embrace all subjects on which precepts were required, and who believed those laws
to be a direct emanation from the Supreme Being. But other nations,
and in particular the Greeks and Romans, who knew that their laws
had been made originally, and still continued to be made, by men,
were not afraid to admit that those men might make bad laws; might
do, by law, the same things, and from the same motives, which,
if done by individuals without the sanction of law, would be called
unjust. And hence the sentiment of injustice came to be attached,
not to all violations of law, but only to violations of such laws as
ought to exist, including such as ought to exist but do not; and to
laws themselves, if supposed to be contrary to what ought to be
law. In this manner the idea of law and of its injunctions was still
predominant in the notion of justice, even when the laws actually
in force ceased to be accepted as the standard of it.

It is true that mankind consider the idea of justice and its obligations as applicable to many things which neither are, nor is it desired
that they should be, regulated by law. Nobody desires that laws
should interfere with the whole detail of private life; yet every one
allows that in all daily conduct a person may and does show himself
to be either just or unjust. But even here, the idea of the breach of

12

13

Circle the word *hence.* This, of
course, is a word signaling that a
conclusion follows.
Mill's conclusion in this paragraph

is ——————————————.

what ought to be law, still lingers in a modified shape. It would always give us pleasure, and chime in with our feelings of fitness, that acts which we deem unjust should be punished, though we do not always think it expedient that this should be done by the tribunals. We forego that gratification on account of incidental inconveniences. We should be glad to see just conduct enforced and injustice repressed, even in the minutest details, if we were not, with reason, afraid of trusting the magistrate with so unlimited an amount of power over individuals. When we think that a person is bound in justice to do a thing, it is an ordinary form of language to say, that he ought to be compelled to do it. We should be gratified to see the obligation enforced by anybody who had the power. If we see that its enforcement by law would be inexpedient, we lament the impossibility, we consider the impunity given to injustice as an evil, and strive to make amends for it by bringing a strong expression of our own and the public disapprobation to bear upon the offender. Thus the idea of legal constraint is still the generating idea of the notion of justice, though undergoing several transformations before that notion, as it exists in an advanced state of society, becomes complete.

14

The above is, I think, a true account, as far as it goes, of the origin and progressive growth of the idea of justice. But we must observe, that it contains, as yet, nothing to distinguish that obligation in general. For the truth is, that the idea of penal sanction, which is the essence of law, enters not only into the conception of injustice, but into that of any kind of wrong. We do not call anything wrong, unless we mean to imply that a person ought to be punished in some way or other for doing it; if not by law, by the opinion of his fellow creatures; if not by opinion, by the reproaches of his own conscience. This seems the real turning point of the distinction between morality and simple expediency. It is a part of the notion of Duty in every one of its forms, that a person may rightfully be compelled to fulfill it. Duty is a thing which may be *exacted* from a person, as one exacts a debt. Unless we think that it might be exacted from him, we do not call it his duty. Reasons of prudence, or the interest of other people, may militate against actually exacting it; but the person himself, it is clearly understood, would not be entitled to complain. There are other things, on the contrary, which we wish that people should do, which we like or admire them for doing, perhaps dislike or despise them for not doing, but yet admit that they are not bound to do; it is not a case of moral obligation; we do not blame them, that is, we do not think that they are proper objects of punishment. How we come by these ideas of deserving and not deserving punishment, will appear, perhaps, in the sequel; but I think there is no doubt that this distinction lies at the bottom of the notions of right and wrong; that we call any conduct wrong, or employ, instead,

Circle the word *thus*. This word often signals that a conclusion will follow.
Mill's conclusion in this paragraph

is _____ .

Circle the word *but*. This word often signals that different or contrasting material will follow. Mill says here that "this is true about

law and justice, but _____

_____ ."

"This distinction" refers to _____

_____ .

some other term of dislike or disparagement, according as we think that the person ought, or ought not, to be punished for it; and we say that it would be right to do so and so, or merely that it would be desirable or laudable, according as we would wish to see the person whom it concerns, compelled, or only persuaded and exhorted, to act in that manner.*

This, therefore, being the characteristic difference which marks off, not justice, but morality in general, from the remaining provinces of Expediency and Worthiness; the character is still to be sought which distinguishes justice from other branches of morality. Now it is known that ethical writers divide moral duties into two classes, denoted by the ill-chosen expressions, duties of perfect and of imperfect obligation; the latter being those in which, though the act is obligatory, the particular occasions of performing it are left to our choice; as in the case of charity or beneficence, which we are indeed bound to practice, but not towards any definite person, nor at any prescribed time. In the more precise language of philosophic jurists, duties of perfect obligation are those duties in virtue of which a correlative *right* resides in some person or persons; duties of imperfect obligation are those moral obligations which do not give birth to any right. I think it will be found that this distinction exactly coincides with that which exists between justice and the other obligations of morality. In our survey of the various popular acceptations of justice, the term appeared generally to involve the idea of a personal right—a claim on the part of one or more individuals, like that which the law gives when if confers a proprietary or other legal right. Whether the injustice consists in depriving a person of a possession, or in breaking faith with him, or in treating him worse than he deserves, or worse than other people who have no greater claims, in each case the supposition implies two things—a wrong done, and some assignable person who is wronged. Injustice may also be done by treating a person better than others; but the wrong in this case is to his competitors, who are also assignable persons. It seems to me that this feature in the case—a right in some person, correlative to the moral obligation—constitutes the specific difference between justice, and generosity or beneficence. Justice implies something which it is not only right to do, and wrong not to do, but which some individual person can claim from us as his moral right. No one has a moral right to our generosity or beneficience, because we are not morally bound to practice those virtues towards any given

15

The difference between duties of perfect and imperfect obligation is

_____.

Underline the sentence beginning ''I think it will be found. . . .'' Mill is limiting the idea of justice.

Underline the sentence beginning ''Justice implies something. . . .'' Mill continues to describe and limit justice.

_____

*See this point enforced and illustrated by Professor Bain, in an admirable chapter (entitled ''The Ethical Emotions, or the Moral Sense''), of the second of the two treatises composing his elaborate and profound work on the Mind. [Alexander Bain. *The Emotions and the Will*. London: Parker, 1859.]

individual. And it will be found with respect to this as with respect to every correct definition, that the instances which seem to conflict with it are those which most confirm it. For if a moralist attempts, as some have done, to make out that mankind generally, though not any given individual, have a right to all the good we can do them, he at once, by that thesis, includes generosity and beneficence within the category of justice. He is obliged to say, that our utmost exertions are *due* to our fellow creatures, thus assimilating them to a debt; or that nothing less can be a sufficient *return* for what society does for us, thus classing the case as one of gratitude; both of which are acknowledged cases of justice. Wherever there is a right, the case is one of justice, and not of the virtue of beneficence: and whoever does not place the distinction between justice and morality in general where we have now placed it, will be found to make no distinction between them at all, but to merge all morality in justice.

Having thus endeavored to determine the distinctive elements which enter into the composition of the idea of justice, we are ready to enter on the inquiry, whether the feeling, which accompanies the idea, is attached to it by a special dispensation of nature, or whether it could have grown up, by any known laws, out of the idea itself; and in particular, whether it can have originated in considerations of general expediency. 16

"The inquiry" that Mill is ready to undertake is _____ .

I conceive that the sentiment itself does not arise from anything which would commonly, or correctly, be termed an idea of expediency; but that though the sentiment does not, whatever is moral in it does. 17

We have seen that the two essential ingredients in the sentiment of justice are, the desire to punish a person who has done harm, and the knowledge or belief that there is some definite individual or individuals to whom harm has been done. 18

The two essential ingredients in the sentiment of justice are _____ _____ and _____ .

Now it appears to me, that the desire to punish a person who has done harm to some individual, is a spontaneous outgrowth from two sentiments, both in the highest degree natural, and which either are or resemble instincts; the impulse of self-defense, and the feeling of sympathy. 19

Underline "the impulse of self-defense, and the feeling of sympathy." Mill describes the two sentiments behind the desire to punish.

Mill has distilled two essential components of justice. The first component of justice is _____ . The second component of justice is _____ . Do you agree with Mill here?

I _____ with Mill because _____

_____

_____
_____
_____ .

It is natural to resent, and to repel or retaliate, any harm done or attempted against ourselves, or against those with whom we sympathize. The origin of this sentiment it is not necessary here to discuss. Whether it be an instinct or a result of intelligence, it is, we know, common to all animal nature; for every animal tries to hurt those who have hurt, or who it thinks are about to hurt, itself or its young. Human beings, on this point, only differ from other animals in two particulars. First, in being capable of sympathizing, not solely with their offspring, or, like some of the more noble animals, with some superior animal who is kind to them, but with all human, and even with all sentient, beings. Secondly, in having a more developed intelligence, which gives a wider range to the whole of their sentiments, whether self-regarding or sympathetic. By virtue of his superior intelligence, even apart from his superior range of sympathy, a human being is capable of apprehending a community of interest between himself and the human society of which he forms a part, such that any conduct which threatens the security of the society generally, is threatening to his own, and calls forth his instinct (if instinct it be) of self-defense. The same superiority of intelligence, joined to the power of sympathizing with human beings generally, enables him to attach himself to the collective idea of his tribe, his country, or mankind, in such a manner that any act hurtful to them rouses his instinct of sympathy, and urges him to resistance.

The sentiment of justice, in that one of its elements which consists of the desire to punish, is thus, I conceive, the natural feeling of retaliation or vengeance, rendered by intellect and sympathy applicable to those injuries, that is, to those hurts, which wound us through, or in common with, society at large. This sentiment, in itself, has nothing moral in it; what is moral is, the exclusive subordination of it to the social sympathies, so as to wait on and obey their call. For the natural feeling tends to make us resent indiscriminately whatever anyone does that is disagreeable to us; but when moralized by the social feeling, it only acts in the directions conformable to the general good: just persons resenting a hurt to society, though not otherwise a hurt to themselves, and not resenting a hurt to themselves, however painful, unless it be of the kind which society has a common interest with them in the repression of.

It is no objection against this doctrine to say, that when we feel our sentiment of justice outraged, we are not thinking of society

20

Underline the two differences between humans and animals mentioned in this paragraph.

Other examples of "collective ideas" besides "tribe, country, and mankind" are first, _____,

and second, _____ .

21

22

at large, or of any collective interest, but only of the individual case. It is common enough certainly, though the reverse of commendable, to feel resentment merely because we have suffered pain; but a person whose resentment is really a moral feeling, that is, who considers whether an act is blameable before he allows himself to resent it—such a person, though he may not say expressly to himself that he is standing up for the interest of society, certainly does feel that he is asserting a rule which is for the benefit of others as well as for his own. If he is not feeling this—if he is regarding the act solely as it affects him individually—he is not consciously just; he is not concerning himself about the justice of his actions. This is admitted even by anti-utilitarian moralists. When Kant (as before remarked) propounds as the fundamental principle of morals, ''So act, that thy rule of conduct might be adopted as a law by all rational beings,'' he virtually acknowledges that the interest of mankind collectively, or at least of mankind indiscriminately, must be in the mind of the agent when conscientiously deciding on the morality of the act. Otherwise he uses words without a meaning: for, that a rule even of utter selfishness could not *possibly* be adopted by all rational beings—that there is any insuperable obstacle in the nature of things to its adoption—cannot be even plausibly maintained. To give any meaning to Kant's principle, the sense put upon it must be, that we ought to shape our conduct by a rule which all rational beings might adopt *with benefit to their collective interest.*

To recapitulate: the idea of justice supposes two things; a rule of conduct, and a sentiment which sanctions the rule. The first must be supposed common to all mankind, and intended for their good. The other (the sentiment) is a desire that punishment may be suffered by those who infringe the rule. There is involved, in addition, the conception of some definite person who suffers by the infringement; whose rights (to use the expression appropriated to the case) are violated by it. And the sentiment of justice appears to me to be, the animal desire to repel or retaliate a hurt or damage to oneself, or to those with whom one sympathizes, widened so as to include all persons, by the human capacity of enlarged sympathy, and the human conception of intelligent self-interest. From the latter elements, the feeling derives its morality; from the former, its peculiar impressiveness, and energy of self-assertion. 23

I have, throughout, treated the idea of a *right* residing in the injured person, and violated by the injury, not as a separate element in the composition of the idea and sentiment, but as one of the forms in which the other two elements clothe themselves. These elements are, a hurt to some assignable person or persons on the one hand, and a demand for punishment on the other. An examination of our own minds, I think, will show, that these two things include all that 24

Underline Kant's fundamental principle of morality. You read a version of this in Chapter 1.

According to Mill, even Kant's ethic acknowledges the _____ _____ interest.

This is a summary paragraph. Read it slowly, several times.

we mean when we speak of violation of a right. When we call anything a person's right, we mean that he has a valid claim on society to protect him in the possession of it, either by the force of law, or by that of education and opinion. If he has what we consider a sufficient claim, on whatever account, to have something guaranteed to him by society, we say that he has a right to it. If we desire to prove that anything does not belong to him by right, we think this done as soon as it is admitted that society ought not to take measures for securing it to him, but should leave it to chance, or to his own exertions. Thus, a person is said to have a right to what he can earn in fair professional competition; because society ought not to allow any other person to hinder him from endeavoring to earn in that manner as much as he can. But he has not a right to three hundred a year, though he may happen to be earning it; because society is not called on to provide that he shall earn that sum. On the contrary, if he owns ten thousand pounds three percent stock, he *has* a right to three hundred a year; because society has come under an obligation to provide him with an income of that amount.

What is meant by a "violation of a right"?

To have a right, then, is, I conceive, to have something which society ought to defend me in the possession of. If the objector goes on to ask why it ought, I can give him no other reason than general utility. If that expression does not seem to convey a sufficient feeling of the strength of the obligation, nor to account for the peculiar energy of the feeling, it is because there goes to the composition of the sentiment, not a rational only but also an animal element, the thirst for retaliation; and this thirst derives its intensity, as well as its moral justification, from the extraordinarily important and impressive kind of utility which is concerned. The interest involved is that of security, to every one's feelings the most vital of all interests. Nearly all other earthly benefits are needed by one person, not needed by another; and many of them can, if necessary, be cheerfully foregone, or replaced by something else; but security no human being can possibly do without; on it we depend for all our immunity from evil, and for the whole value of all and every good, beyond the passing moment; since nothing but the gratification of the instant could be of any worth to us, if we could be deprived of everything the next instant by whoever was momentarily stronger than ourselves. Now this most indispensable of all necessaries, after physical nutriment, cannot be had, unless the machinery for providing it is kept unintermittedly in active play. Our notion, therefore, of the claim we have on our fellow creatures to join in making safe for us the groundwork of our existence, gathers feelings round it so much more intense than those concerned in any of the more common cases of utility, that the difference in degree (as is often

25
Underline the first two sentences in this paragraph. Mill's argument again circles back to the notion of utility.

Society ought to defend the possession of something because

_____ .

the case in psychology) becomes a real difference in kind. The claim assumes that character of absoluteness, that apparent infinity, and incommensurability with all other considerations, which constitute the distinction between the feeling of right and wrong and that of ordinary expediency and inexpediency. The feelings concerned are so powerful, and we count so positively on finding a responsive feeling in others (all being alike interested), that *ought* and *should* grow into *must,* and recognised indispensability becomes a moral necessity, analogous to physical, and often not inferior to it in binding force.

If the preceding analysis, or something resembling it, be not 26 the correct account of the notion of justice; if justice be totally independent of utility, and be a standard *per se,*[9] which the mind can recognize by simple introspection of itself; it is hard to understand why that internal oracle is so ambiguous, and why so many things appear either just or unjust, according to the light in which they are regarded.

We are continually informed that Utility is an uncertain standard, 27 which every different person interprets differently, and that there is no safety but in the immutable, ineffaceable, and unmistakable dictates of Justice, which carry their evidence in themselves, and are independent of the fluctuations of opinion. One would suppose from this that on questions of justice there could be no controversy; that if we take that for our rule, its application to any given case could leave us in as little doubt as a mathematical demonstration. So far is this from being the fact, that there is as much difference of opinion, and as fierce discussion, about what is just, as about what is useful to society. Not only have different nations and individuals different notions of justice, but, in the mind of one and the same individual, justice is not some one rule, principle, or maxim, but many, which do not always coincide in their dictates, and in choosing between which, he is guided either by some extraneous standard, or by his own personal predilections.

"That internal oracle" refers to

_____.

Is Mill saying that justice is independent of utility or dependent on utility?

Justice is _____ utility. Reread the paragraph slowly. Mill introduces the next major idea at the end of this paragraph.

A criticism of utilitarianism has been

that _____. For these

critics, the idea of _____ is constant and unchanging. Underline the sentence beginning "So far is this from . . ." Here Mill argues that justice has many interpretations.

Mill develops his argument. Were you right in your anticipation? Mill connects justice and utility. Justice is not distinct and unambiguous; there are many theories of justice. His example will be punishment for a crime.

Most people are punished for crimes because _____

_____

_____.

Is punishment a form of rehabilitation? _____ . I say this

because _____

_____

_____.

Are people responsible for their actions if society deforms and distorts them? People _____ responsible in such situations because _____

_____

_____.

For instance, there are some who say, that it is unjust to punish anyone for the sake of example to others; that punishment is just, only when intended for the good of the sufferer himself. Others maintain the extreme reverse, contending that to punish persons who have attained years of discretion, for their own benefit, is despotism and injustice, since if the matter at issue is solely their own good, no one has a right to control their own judgment of it; but that they may justly be punished to prevent evil to others, this being an exercise of the legitimate right of self-defense. Mr. Owen,[10] again, affirms that it is unjust to punish at all; for the criminal did not make his own character; his education, and the circumstances which surround him, have made him a criminal, and for these he is not responsible. All these opinions are extremely plausible; and so long as the question is argued as one of justice simply, without going down to the principles which lie under justice and are the source of its authority, I am unable to see how any of these reasoners can be refuted. For, in truth, every one of the three builds upon rules of justice confessedly true. The first appeals to the acknowledged injustice of singling out an individual, and making him a sacrifice, without his consent, for other people's benefit. The second relies on the acknowledged justice of self-defense, and the admitted injustice of forcing one person to conform to another's notions of what constitutes his good. The Owenite invokes the admitted principle, that it is unjust to punish anyone for what he cannot help. Each is triumphant so long as he is not compelled to take into consideration any other maxims of justice than the one he has selected; but as soon as their several maxims are brought face to face, each disputant seems to have exactly as much to say for himself as the others. No one of them can carry out his own notion of justice without trampling upon another equally binding. These are difficulties; they have always been felt to be such; and many devices have been invented to turn rather than to overcome them. As a refuge from the last of the three, men imagined what they called

28
Circle the phrase "For instance." This introduces an example.

the freedom of the will; fancying that they could not justify punishing a man whose will is in a thoroughly hateful state, unless it be supposed to have come into that state through no influence of anterior circumstances. To escape from the other difficulties, a favorite contrivance has been the fiction of a contract, whereby at some unknown period all the members of society engaged to obey the laws, and consented to be punished for any disobedience to them; thereby giving to their legislators the right, which it is assumed they would not otherwise have had, of punishing them, either for their own good or for that of society. This happy thought was considered to get rid of the whole difficulty, and to legitimate the infliction of punishment, in virtue of another received maxim of justice, *volenti non fit injuria;*[*][11] that is not unjust which is done with the consent of the person who is supposed to be hurt by it. I need hardly remark, that even if the consent were not a mere fiction, this maxim is not superior in authority to the others which it is brought in to supersede. It is, on the contrary, an instructive specimen of the loose and irregular manner in which supposed principles of justice grow up. This particular one evidently came into use as a help to the coarse exigencies of courts of law, which are sometimes obliged to be content with very uncertain presumptions, on account of the greater evils which would often arise from any attempt on their part to cut finer. But even courts of law are not able to adhere consistently to the maxim, for they allow voluntary engagements to be set aside on the ground of fraud, and sometimes on that of mere mistake or misinformation.

Again, when the legitimacy of inflicting punishment is admitted, how many conflicting conceptions of justice come to light in discussing the proper apportionment of punishment to offenses. No rule on this subject recommends itself so strongly to the primitive and spontaneous sentiment of justice, as the *lex talionis,*[12] an eye for an eye and a tooth for a tooth. Though this principle of the Jewish and of the Mohamedan[13] law has been generally abandoned in Europe as a practical maxim, there is, I suspect, in most minds, a secret hankering after it; and when retribution accidentally falls on an offender in that precise shape, the general feeling of satisfaction evinced, bears witness how natural is the sentiment to which this repayment in kind is acceptable. With many the test of justice in penal infliction is that the punishment should be proportioned to the offense; meaning that it should be exactly measured by the moral guilt of the culprit (whatever be their standard for measuring moral guilt): the consideration, what amount of punishment is necessary to deter from the offense, having nothing to do with the question

29

[*See Ulpian. *Corpus Juris Civilis Romani, Digesta.* Lib. XLVII, Tit. x, 1, §5.]

of justice, in their estimation: while there are others to whom that consideration is all in all; who maintain that it is not just, at least for man, to inflict on a fellow creature, whatever may be his offenses, any amount of suffering beyond the least that will suffice to prevent him from repeating, and others from imitating, his misconduct.

To take another example from a subject already once referred to. In a co-operative industrial association, is it just or not that talent or skill should give a title to superior remuneration? On the negative side of the question it is argued, that whoever does the best he can, deserves equally well, and ought not in justice to be put in a position of inferiority for no fault of his own; that superior abilities have already advantages more than enough, in the admiration they excite, the personal influence they command, and the internal sources of satisfaction attending them, without adding to these a superior share of the world's goods; and that society is bound in justice rather to make compensation to the less favored, for this unmerited inequality of advantages, than to aggravate it. On the contrary side it is contended, that society receives more from the more efficient laborer; that his services being more useful, society owes him a larger return for them; that a greater share of the joint result is actually his work, and not to allow his claim to it is a kind of robbery; that if he is only to receive as much as others, he can only be justly required to produce as much, and to give a smaller amount of time and exertion, proportioned to his superior efficiency. Who shall decide between these appeals to conflicting principles of justice? Justice has in this case two sides to it, which it is impossible to bring into harmony, and the two disputants have chosen opposite sides; the one looks to what it is just that the individual should receive, the other to what it is just that the community should give. Each, from his own point of view, is unanswerable; and any choice between them, on grounds of justice, must be perfectly arbitrary. Social utility alone can decide the preference.

How many, again, and how irreconcileable, are the standards of justice to which reference is made in discussing the repartition of taxation. One opinion is, that payment to the State should be in numerical proportion to pecuniary means. Others think that justice dictates what they term graduated taxation; taking a higher percentage from those who have more to spare. In point of natural justice a strong case might be made for disregarding means altogether, and taking the same absolute sum (whenever it could be got) from every one: as the subscribers to a mess, or to a club, all pay the same sum for the same privileges, whether they can all equally afford it or not. Since the protection (it might be said) of law and government is afforded to, and is equally required by, all, there is no injustice in making all buy it at the same price. It is reckoned justice, not injustice, that a dealer should charge to all customers the same

30

Circle the phrase "take another example." Mill builds his argument by using a series of examples.

Underline the sentence beginning "In a co-operative industrial. . . ." This question identifies the example Mill will use.

What do you think will be Mill's answer?

Mill will say that _____.

Underline the last two sentences of this paragraph. They restate Mill's theme.

31

The next example deals with _____
_____.

price for the same article, not a price varying according to their means of payment. This doctrine, as applied to taxation, finds no advocates, because it conflicts strongly with men's feelings of humanity and perception of social expediency; but the principle of justice which it invokes is as true and as binding as those which can be appealed to against it. Accordingly, it exerts a tacit influence on the line of defense employed for other modes of assessing taxation. People feel obliged to argue that the State does more for the rich than for the poor, as a justification for its taking more from them: though this is in reality not true, for the rich would be far better able to protect themselves, in the absence of law or government, than the poor, and indeed would probably be successful in converting the poor into their slaves. Others, again, so far defer to the same conception of justice, as to maintain that all should pay an equal capitation tax for the protection of their persons (these being of equal value to all), and an unequal tax for the protection of their property, which is unequal. To this others reply, that the all of one man is as valuable to him as the all of another. From these confusions there is no other mode of extrication than the utilitarian.

Is, then, the difference between the Just and the Expedient a merely imaginary distinction? Have mankind been under a delusion in thinking that justice is a more sacred thing than policy, and that the latter ought only to be listened to after the former has been satisfied? By no means. The exposition we have given of the nature and origin of the sentiment, recognises a real distinction; and no one of those who profess the most sublime contempt for the consequences of actions as an element in their morality, attaches more importance to the distinction than I do. While I dispute the pretensions of any theory which sets up an imaginary standard of justice not grounded on utility, I account the justice which is grounded on utility to be the chief part, and incomparably the most sacred and binding part, of all morality. Justice is a name for certain classes of moral rules, which concern the essentials of human well-being more nearly, and are therefore of more absolute obligation, than any other rules for the guidance of life; and the notion which we have found to be of the essence of the idea of justice, that of a right residing in an individual, implies and testifies to this more binding obligation. 32

The moral rules which forbid mankind to hurt one another (in which we must never forget to include wrongful interference with each other's freedom) are more vital to human well-being than any maxims, however important, which only point out the best mode of managing some department of human affairs. They have also the peculiarity, that they are the main element in determining the whole of the social feelings of mankind. It is their observance which alone preserves peace among human beings: if obedience to them were not the rule, and disobedience the exception, every one would see 33

Underline the sentence beginning "While I dispute. . . ." Justice,

grounded on _____,
is the chief part of all morality.

What Mill is saying here is_____
_____ .

in every one else a probable enemy, against whom he must be perpetually guarding himself. What is hardly less important, these are the precepts which mankind have the strongest and the most direct inducements for impressing upon one another. By merely giving to each other prudential instruction or exhortation, they may gain, or think they gain, nothing: in inculcating on each other the duty of positive beneficence they have an unmistakable interest, but far less in degree: a person may possibly not need the benefits of others; but he always needs that they should not do him hurt. Thus the moralities which protect every individual from being harmed by others, either directly or by being hindered in his freedom of pursuing his own good, are at once those which he himself has most at heart, and those which he has the strongest interest in publishing and enforcing by word and deed. It is by a person's observance of these, that his fitness to exist as one of the fellowship of human beings, is tested and decided; for on that depends his being a nuisance or not to those with whom he is in contact. Now it is these moralities primarily, which compose the obligations of justice. The most marked cases of injustice, and those which give the tone to the feeling of repugnance which characterizes the sentiment, are acts of wrongful aggression, or wrongful exercise of power over some one; the next are those which consist in wrongfully withholding from him something which is his due; in both cases, inflicting on him a positive hurt, either in the form of direct suffering, or of the privation of some good which he had reasonable ground, either of a physical or of a social kind, for counting upon.

"These moralities" refers to _____

_____ .

The same powerful motives which command the observance of these primary moralities, enjoin the punishment of those who violate them; and as the impulses of self-defense, of defense of others, and of vengeance, are all called forth against such persons, retribution, or evil for evil, becomes closely connected with the sentiment of justice, and is universally included in the idea. Good for good is also one of the dictates of justice; and this, though its social utility is evident, and though it carries with it a natural human feeling, has not at first sight that obvious connection with hurt or injury, which, existing in the most elementary cases of just and unjust, is the source of the characteristic intensity of the sentiment. But the connection, though less obvious, is not less real. He who accepts benefits, and denies a return of them when needed, inflicts a real hurt, by disappointing one of the most natural and reasonable of expectations, and one which he must at least tacitly have encouraged, otherwise the benefits would seldom have been conferred. The important rank, among human evils and wrongs, of the disappointment of expectation, is shown in the fact that it constitutes the principal criminality of two such highly immoral acts as a breach of friendship and a breach of promise. Few hurts which human

34

beings can sustain are greater, and none wound more, than when that on which they habitually and with full assurance relied, fails them in the hour of need; and few wrongs are greater than this mere withholding of good; none excite more resentment, either in the person suffering, or in a sympathizing spectator. The principle, therefore, of giving to each what they deserve, that is, good for good as well as evil for evil, is not only included within the idea of Justice as we have defined it, but is a proper object of that intensity of sentiment, which places the Just, in human estimation, above the simply Expedient.

Most of the maxims of justice current in the world, and 35 commonly appealed to in its transactions, are simply instrumental to carrying into effect the principles of justice which we have now spoken of. That a person is only responsible for what he has done voluntarily, or could voluntarily have avoided; that it is unjust to condemn any person unheard; that the punishment ought to be proportioned to the offense, and the like, are maxims intended to prevent the just principle of evil for evil from being perverted to the infliction of evil without that justification. The greater part of these common maxims have come into use from the practice of courts of justice, which have been naturally led to a more complete recognition and elaboration than was likely to suggest itself to others, of the rules necessary to enable them to fulfill their double function, of inflicting punishment when due, and of awarding to each person his right.

That first of judicial virtues, impartiality, is an obligation of 36 justice, partly for the reason last mentioned; as being a necessary condition of the fulfillment of the other obligations of justice. But this is not the only source of the exalted rank, among human obligations, of those maxims of equality and impartiality, which, both in popular estimation and in that of the most enlightened, are included among the precepts of justice. In one point of view, they may be considered as corollaries from the principles already laid down. If it is a duty to do to each according to his deserts, returning good for good as well as repressing evil by evil, it necessarily follows that we should treat all equally well (when no higher duty forbids) who have deserved equally well of us, and that society should treat all equally well who have deserved equally well of it, that is, who have deserved equally well absolutely. This is the highest abstract standard of social and distributive justice; towards which all institutions, and the efforts of all virtuous citizens, should be made in the utmost possible degree to converge. But this great moral duty rests upon a still deeper foundation, being a direct emanation from the first principle of morals, and not a mere logical corollary from secondary or derivative doctrines. It is involved in the very meaning of Utility, or the Greatest-Happiness Principle. That principle is a mere form

Underline the two sentences beginning ''But this great moral duty. . . .'' Mill emphasizes the principle of utility as the principle of morality.

of words without rational signification, unless one person's happiness, supposed equal in degree (with the proper allowance made for kind), is counted for exactly as much as another's. Those conditions being supplied, Bentham's dictum, "everybody to count for one, nobody for more than one," might be written under the principle of utility as an explanatory commentary. The equal claim of everybody to happiness in the estimation of the moralist and the legislator, involves an equal claim to all the means of happiness, except in so far as the inevitable conditions of human life, and the general interest, in which that of every individual is included, set limits to the maxim; and those limits ought to be strictly construed. As every other maxim of justice, so this, is by no means applied or held applicable universally; on the contrary, as I have already remarked, it bends to every person's ideas of social expediency. But in whatever case it is deemed applicable at all, it is held to be the dictate of justice. All persons are deemed to have a *right* to equality of treatment, except when some recognised social expediency requires the reverse. And hence all social inequalities which have ceased to be considered expedient, assume the character not of simple inexpediency, but of injustice, and appear so tyrannical, that people are apt to wonder how they ever could have been tolerated; forgetful that they themselves perhaps tolerate other inequalities under an equally mistaken notion of expediency, the correction of which would make that which they approve seem quite as monstrous as what they have at last learned to condemn. The entire history of social improvement has been a series of transitions, by which one custom or institution after another, from being a supposed primary necessity of social existence, has passed into the rank of an universally stigmatized injustice and tyranny. So it has been with the distinctions of slaves and freemen, nobles and serfs, patricians and plebeians; and so it will be, and in part already is, with the aristocracies of color, race, and sex.

The three examples of injustice and tyranny given by Mill from his own experience are: (1) _____ _____; (2) _____; and (3) _____. 37

It appears from what has been said, that justice is a name for certain moral requirements, which, regarded collectively, stand higher in the scale of social utility, and are therefore of more paramount obligation, than any others; though particular cases may occur in which some other social duty is so important, as to overrule any one of the general maxims of justice. Thus, to save a life, it may not only be allowable, but a duty, to steal, or take by force, the necessary food or medicine, or to kidnap, and compel to officiate, the only qualified medical practitioner. In such cases, as we do not call anything justice which is not a virtue, we usually say, not that justice must give way to some other moral principle, but that what is just in ordinary cases is, by reason of that other principle, not just in the particular case. By this useful accommodation of language, the character of indefeasibility attributed to justice is kept up, and we are saved from the necessity of maintaining that there can be laudable injustice.

The considerations which have now been adduced resolve, I 38 conceive, the only real difficulty in the utilitarian theory of morals. It has always been evident that all cases of justice are also cases of expediency: the difference is in the peculiar sentiment which attaches to the former, as contradistinguished from the latter. If this characteristic sentiment has been sufficiently accounted for; if there is no necessity to assume for it any peculiarity of origin; if it is simply the natural feeling of resentment, moralized by being made co-extensive with the demands of social good; and if this feeling not only does but ought to exist in all the classes of cases to which ''That idea'' refers to _____ . the idea of justice corresponds; that idea no longer presents itself as a stumbling-block to the utilitarian ethics. Justice remains the appropriate name for certain social utilities which are vastly more important, and therefore more absolute and imperative, than any others are as a class (though not more so than others may be in particular cases); and which, therefore, ought to be, as well as naturally are, guarded by a sentiment not only different in degree, but also in kind; distinguished from the milder feeling which attaches to the mere idea of promoting human pleasure or convenience, at once by the more definite nature of its commands, and by the sterner character of its sanctions.

Your best friend appears. She wants to know how your studies have been going. Tell her your reactions to reading John Stuart Mill's *Utilitarianism.*
The most important thing I learned about ethics from reading this

text was _____

_____

_____

_____ .

I can best describe my reactions to this work with the word

_____ . I chose this word because _____

_____

_____

_____ .

In the Preface, we quoted another philosopher who spoke of *vertical* and *horizontal* reading. When you read horizontally, you will go from here and read other things by Mill, about ethics, in philosophy, regarding social criticism. This is good. But you can also read vertically. That means going back to the beginning—in a week, a month, a year or two, a decade—and rereading what you have just read. Classics are "bottomless"; you never get to the bottom—the meaning—because the reading changes every time.

Before you end this guided tour, the journey, there is one more task. When you travel, you sometimes learn helpful hints about the process—pack lighter, do not pack liquids, never forget an extra pair of glasses, always eat breakfast, and so on. You have been on a philosophical journey. What have you learned about such a journey? What one piece of advice would you give a fellow traveller as she or he undertook such a journey?

I would say to a fellow traveller on such a philosophical journey

_____

_____

_____

_____

_____.

Whether you move horizontally or vertically from here, good luck on your travels.

Notes

1. *Sui generis* is a Latin phrase meaning "of its own kind," unique, peculiar, constituting a class in itself.

2. Since Mill wrote before Lenin, and thus before the birth of twentieth-century communism, do not associate this reference with contemporary political movements. This term refers to those thinkers who advocate a variety of communal life styles.

3. Etymology is the study of the origin and the history of words.

4. *Justum* is the Latin root of Justice.

5. *Dikaion* is Greek.

6. *Dike* is Greek.

7. *Recht* is German.

8. *Droit* is French.

9. *Per se* is Latin for by, of, in, or for itself; as such; intrinsically.

10. Robert Owen (1771–1858 C.E.) developed a view of modified communism in his *New Vision of Society*. He was active in establishing labor leagues in England.

11. *Volenti non fit injuria* is a Latin phrase stating that merely willing something does not cause harm.

12. *Lex talionis* is a Latin phrase meaning "law of the talon." This is a reference to the biblical passage that includes "an eye for an eye, a tooth for a tooth." In its original context, however, this law of revenge and retaliation was a merciful attempt to prevent disproportionate reaction to particular events.

13. *Mohamedan* is Mill's word for the follower of the religion of Islam. This word is not an accurate or helpful description. A follower of Islam would properly be called a Muslim. The adjective for Islam is *Islamic*.

PART 3
Other Readings from the Utilitarian Tradition

As was mentioned in the Introduction, the ideas in *Utilitarianism* belong to a long history in philosophy where the right or good thing to do is based on the criteria of pleasure and pain. A reading selection by Epicurus will give you an ancient classical statement of this tradition, while the selection by Bentham will give you an example from the era of J. S. Mill.

Epicurus
Letter to Menoeceus

Epicurus (341–270 B.C.E.) lived during the Hellenistic period, where the influence of Greek (Hellenic) culture was spread by the conquests of Alexander the Great. The Greek city-state, the polis, which was the place where morality was nurtured, gave way to an "empire" and to variations on large governmental and administrative structures. If the model for the good life in the polis is gone, where should one look to solve the questions of morality? For Epicurus, the good life is made possible by having the individual focus on pleasure and pain—enjoying the former and avoiding the latter.

Epicureanism has often been used in our culture (and in the culture of J. S. Mill) as a label to refer to a base and crass quest for physical pleasures at all costs. This is *not* the philosophy of Epicurus. Avoiding pain is a component of the good life, and one must sometimes avoid pleasure to avoid the painful consequences of the initially pleasurable action. "Repose"—the quiet, serene enjoyment of simple pleasures—thus becomes a component of the good life. J. S. Mill notes that some critics of his version of utilitarianism use a distorted form of Epicureanism as a support for their arguments. Mill saves Epicurus's ideas and presses their ethical implications a bit further.

The Preconditions of Happiness

I. You should do and practice all the things I constantly recommended to you, with the knowledge that they are the fundamentals of the good life. (1) First of all, you should think of deity as imperishable and blessed being (as delineated in the universal conception of it common to all men), and you should not attribute to it anything foreign to its immortality or inconsistent with its blessedness. On the contrary, you should hold every doctrine that is capable of safeguarding its blessedness in common with its imperishability. The gods do indeed exist, since our knowledge of them is a matter of clear and distinct perception; but they are not like what the masses suppose them to be, because most people do not maintain the pure conception of the gods. The irreligious man is not the person who destroys the gods of the masses but the person who imposes the ideas of the masses on the gods. The opinions held by most people about the gods are not true conceptions of them but fallacious notions, according to which awful penalties are meted out to the evil and the greatest of blessings to the good. The masses, by assimilating the gods in every respect to their own moral qualities, accept deities similar to themselves and regard anything not of this sort as alien.

(2) Second, you should accustom yourself to believing that death means nothing to us, since every good and every evil lies in sensation; but death is the privation of sensation. Hence a correct comprehension of the fact that death means nothing to us makes the mortal aspect of life pleasurable, not by conferring on us a boundless period of time but by removing the yearning for deathlessness. There is nothing fearful in living for the person who has really laid hold of the fact that there is nothing fearful in not living. So it is silly for a person to say that he dreads death—not because it will be painful when it arrives but because it pains him now as a future certainty; for that which makes no trouble for us when it arrives is a meaningless pain when we await it. This, the most horrifying of evils, means nothing to us, then, because so long as we are existent death is not present and whenever it is present we are nonexistent. Thus it is of no concern either to the living or to those who have completed their lives. For the former it is nonexistent, and the latter are themselves nonexistent.

Most people, however, recoil from death as though it were the greatest of evils; at other times they welcome it as the end-all of life's ills. The sophisticated person, on the other hand, neither begs off from living nor dreads not living. Life is not a stumbling block to him, nor does he regard not being alive as any sort of evil. As in the case of food he prefers the most savory dish to merely the larger portion, so in the case of time he garners to himself the most agreeable moments rather than the longest span.

Anyone who urges the youth to lead a good life but counsels the older man to end his life in good style is silly, not merely because of the welcome character of life but because of the fact that living

For Epicurus, the first precondition of happiness has to do with the divine. What reason does he give that the gods (note the plural) exist?

The gods exist because _____

_____

_____ .

A fallacy is an error in reasoning.

Epicurus gives a reason why there is nothing fearful in death. A person may dread death, not because death will be painful but because

_____

_____ .

Death is not to be feared, because as long as people are alive, _____

_____

_____ , and when people are dead, _____

_____ .

well and dying well are one and the same discipline. Much worse off, however, is the person who says it were well not to have been born "but once born to pass Hades' portals as swiftly as may be." Now if he says such a thing from inner persuasion why does he not withdraw from life? Everything is in readiness for him once he has firmly resolved on this course. But if he speaks facetiously he is a trifler standing in the midst of men who do not welcome him.

It should be borne in mind, then, that the time to come is neither ours nor altogether not ours. In this way we shall neither expect the future outright as something destined to be nor despair of it as something absolutely not destined to be.

In this section, Epicurus has argued that there are two preconditions to happiness. The first has to do with _____ _____. The second precondition to happiness deals with _____. Do you agree with Epicurus's assertion that "it is silly for a person to say that he dreads death"? _____. Why or why not? _____ _____ _____ .

The Good Life

Epicurus says that there are two kinds of natural desires. Some natural desires are _____ _____, so natural desires are _____ and _____ .

II. It should be recognized that within the category of desire certain desires are natural, certain others unnecessary and trivial; that in the case of the natural desires certain ones are necessary, certain others merely natural; and that in the case of necessary desires certain ones are necessary for happiness, others to promote freedom from bodily discomfort, others for the maintenance of life itself. A steady view of these matters shows us how to refer all moral choices and aversion to bodily health and imperturbability of mind, these being the twin goals of happy living. It is on this account that we do everything we do—to achieve freedom from pain and freedom from fear. When once we come by this, the tumult in the soul is calmed and the human being does not have to go about looking for something that is lacking or to search for something additional with which to supplement the welfare of soul and body. Accordingly we have need of pleasure only when we feel pain because of the absence of pleasure, but whenever we do not feel pain we no longer stand in need of pleasure. And so we speak of pleasure as the starting point and the goal of the happy life because we realize that it is our primary native good, because every act of choice and aversion

For Epicurus, _____ is the starting point and the goal of the happy life.

originates with it, and because we come back to it when we judge every good by using the pleasure feeling as our criterion.

Because of the very fact that pleasure is our primary and congenital good we do not select every pleasure; there are times when we forgo certain pleasures, particularly when they are followed by too much unpleasantness. Furthermore, we regard certain states of pain as preferable to pleasures, particularly when greater satisfaction results from our having submitted to discomforts for a long period of time. Thus every pleasure is a good by reason of its having a nature akin to our own, but not every pleasure is desirable. In like manner every state of pain is an evil, but not all pains are uniformly to be rejected. At any rate, it is our duty to judge all such cases by measuring pleasures against pains, with a view to their respective assets and liabilities, inasmuch as we do experience the good as being bad at times and, contrariwise, the bad as being good.

In addition, we consider limitation of the appetites a major good, and we recommend this practice not for the purpose of enjoying just a few things and no more but rather for the purpose of enjoying those few in case we do not have much. We are firmly convinced that those who need expensive fare least are the ones who relish it most keenly and that a natural way of life is easily procured, while trivialities are hard to come by. Plain foods afford pleasure equivalent to that of a sumptuous diet, provided that the pains of penury are wholly eliminated. Barley bread and water yield the peak of pleasure whenever a person who needs them sets them in front of himself. Hence becoming habituated to a simple rather than a lavish way of life provides us with the full complement of health; it makes a person ready for the necessary business of life; it puts us in a position of advantage when we happen upon sumptuous fare at intervals and prepares us to be fearless in facing fortune.

Thus when I say that pleasure is the goal of living I do not mean the pleasures of libertines or the pleasures inherent in positive enjoyment, as is supposed by certain persons who are ignorant of our doctrine or who are not in agreement with it or who interpret it perversely. I mean, on the contrary, the pleasure that consists in freedom from bodily pain and mental agitation. The pleasant life is not the product of one drinking party after another or of sexual intercourse with women and boys or of the sea food and other delicacies afforded by a luxurious table. On the contrary, it is the result of sober thinking—namely, investigation of the reasons for every act of choice and aversion and elimination of those false ideas about the gods and death which are the chief source of mental disturbances.

For Epicurus, the good life consists of pleasure and freedom from _____ and

Epicurus would say a person should avoid certain pleasures when

_____

_____ .

By measuring _____
against _____ ,
Epicurus will find the right thing to do.

Hence signals that Epicurus will state a conclusion. In this sentence, he claims that becoming habituated to a simple life does at least three

things. First, it _____

_____ .

Second, it _____

_____ .

Finally, becoming habituated to a

simple life prepares us to _____

_____ .

Underline the sentence beginning ''I mean, on the contrary . . . .'' Note that Epicurus includes ''mental agitation'' as something that disturbs pleasure.

mental _____. In the last sentence he says that the chief sources of mental disturbances are false ideas about _____ and _____.

Do you agree with Epicurus on this point? _____. Why or why not? _____

_____

_____.

Leading Doctrines

1–5: Five Fundamental Teachings Bearing on the Good Life

1. The blessed and indestructible being of the divine has no concerns of its own, nor does it make trouble for others. It is not affected by feelings of anger or benevolence, because these are found where there is lack of strength.

By this assertion, Epicurus is concerned only with what has _____ _____.

Since _____ has no sensation, it is not a concern of his.

2. Death means nothing to us, because that which has been broken down into atoms has no sensation and that which has no sensation is no concern of ours.

3. The quantitative limit of pleasure is the elimination of all feelings of pain. Wherever the pleasurable state exists, there is neither bodily pain nor mental pain nor both together, so long as the state continues.

4. Bodily pain does not last continuously. The peak is present for a very brief period, and pains that barely exceed the state of bodily pleasure do not continue for many days. On the other hand, protracted illnesses show a balance of bodily pleasure over pain.

Living the pleasant life is the same as _____ _____ _____ _____.

5. It is impossible to live the pleasant life without also living sensibly, nobly, and justly, and conversely it is impossible to live sensibly, nobly, and justly without living pleasantly. A person who does not have a pleasant life is not living sensibly, nobly, and justly, and conversely the person who does not have these virtues cannot live pleasantly.

8–9: How to Choose Pleasures

8. No pleasure is bad in itself. But the things that make for pleasure in certain cases entail disturbances many times greater than the pleasures themselves.

9. If all pleasures could be compressed in time and intensity, and were characteristic of the whole man or his more important aspects, the various pleasures would not differ from each other.

26, 29, 30: *Classification of Human Desires*

29. Some desires are (1) natural and necessary, others (2) natural but not necessary, still others (3) neither natural nor necessary but generated by senseless whims.

26. All desires that do not lead to physical pain if not satisfied are unnecessary, and involve cravings that are easily resolved when they appear to entail harm or when the object of desire is hard to get.

30. If interest is intense in the case of those natural desires that do not lead to physical pain when they are not satisfied, then such desires are generated by idle fancy, and it is not because of their own nature that they are not dissipated but because of the person's own senseless whims.

Imagine that you are talking to Epicurus. He asks you for an example of a desire that is natural and necessary. What example would you give him? _____.
Give him an example of a desire that is natural and not necessary.

_____.

Now give him an example of a desire that is neither natural nor necessary but a "senseless whim." _____

_____.

Epicurus says there are three kinds of desires. The first is _____

_____.

The second kind of desire is _____

_____.

The third kind is _____

_____.

Jeremy Bentham
An Introduction to the Principles of Morals and Legislation

Jeremy Bentham (1748–1832 C.E.) constitutes a continuation of the ideas of Epicurus; pleasure and pain are still key elements. But the social situation has changed again. Epicurus reflected the changed Hellenistic culture; Jeremy Bentham mirrors a society in the midst of a scientific revolution. Epicurus's ethics may be called "egoistic"—concerned with the individual—whereas Bentham represents a "social" hedonism. Furthermore, observation and quantification are components of the scientific mentality in Europe from the seventeenth century forward. Bentham sought to find measurable, quantifiable, units to create a moral calculus, a mathematical way of dealing with ethical issues.

John Stuart Mill was deeply influenced by Bentham. Mill served as a critical reader for much of Bentham's later work. But *quantity* was not enough for Mill. He realized that *quality* had to be inserted into the equation. And when this is done, the equation ceases to be mathematical. Ethics takes on a different tone and texture.

Chapter I: Of the Principle of Utility

1. Nature has placed mankind under the governance of two sovereign masters, *pain* and *pleasure.* It is for them alone to point out what we ought to do, as well as to determine what we shall do. On the one hand the standard of right and wrong, on the other the chain of causes and effects, are fastened to their throne. They govern us in all we do, in all we say, in all we think: every effort we can make to throw off our subjection, will serve but to demonstrate and confirm it. In words a man may pretend to abjure their empire: but in reality he will remain subject to it all the while. The *principle of utility* recognises this subjection, and assumes it for the foundation of that system, the object of which is to rear the fabric of felicity by the hands of reason and of law. Systems which attempt to question it, deal in sounds instead of sense, in caprice instead of reason, in darkness instead of light.

Bentham states that the standard of right and wrong is "fastened to the throne" of two "sovereign masters," _____ and _____ .

But enough of metaphor and declamation: it is not by such means that moral science is to be improved.

2. The principle of utility is the foundation of the present work: it will be proper therefore at the outset to give an explicit and determinate account of what is meant by it. By the principle of utility is meant that principle which approves or disapproves of every action whatsoever, according to the tendency which it appears to have to augment or diminish the happiness of the party whose interest is in question: or, what is the same thing in other words, to promote or to oppose that happiness. I say of every action whatsoever; and therefore not only of every action of a private individual, but of every measure of government.

The principle of utility is not only the guide for acts of individuals but also the guide and measure for

_____ .

3. By utility is meant that property in any object, whereby it tends to produce benefit, advantage, pleasure, good, or happiness, (all this in the present case comes to the same thing) or (what comes again to the same thing) to prevent the happening of mischief, pain, evil, or unhappiness to the party whose interest is considered: if that party be the community in general, then the happiness of the community: if a particular individual, then the happiness of that individual.

4. The interest of the community is one of the most general expressions that can occur in the phraseology of morals: no wonder that the meaning of it is often lost. When it has a meaning, it is this. The community is a fictitious *body*, composed of the individual persons who are considered as constituting as it were its *members*. The interest of the community then is, what?—the sum of the interests of the several members who compose it.

Bentham's philosophy is social. The interest of the community is the sum of _____ _____ .

5. It is in vain to talk of the interest of the community, without understanding what is the interest of the individual. A thing is said to promote the interest, or to be *for* the interest, of an individual, when it tends to add to the sum total of his pleasures: or, what comes to the same thing, to diminish the sum total of his pains.

6. An action then may be said to be conformable to the principle of utility, or, for shortness sake, to utility, (meaning with respect to the community at large) when the tendency it has to augment the happiness of the community is greater than any it has to diminish it.

7. A measure of government (which is but a particular kind of action, performed by a particular person or persons) may be said to be conformable to or dictated by the principle of utility, when in like manner the tendency which it has to augment the happiness of the community is greater than any which it has to diminish it.

8. When an action, or in particular a measure of government, is supposed by a man to be conformable to the principle of utility, it may be convenient, for the purposes of discourse, to imagine a kind of law or dictate, called a law or dictate of utility: and to speak of the action in question, as being conformable to such law or dictate.

9. A man may be said to be a partisan of the principle of utility, when the approbation or disapprobation he annexes to any action, or to any measure, is determined by, and proportioned to the tendency which he conceives it to have to augment or to diminish the happiness of the community: or in other words, to its conformity or unconformity to the laws or dictates of utility.

10. Of an action that is conformable to the principle of utility, one may always say either that it is one that ought to be done, or at least that it is not one that ought not to be done. One may say also, that it is right it should be done; at least that it is not wrong it should be done: that it is a right action; at least that it is not a wrong action. When thus interpreted, the words *ought,* and *right* and *wrong,* and others of that stamp, have a meaning: when otherwise, they have none.

11. Has the rectitude of this principle been ever formally contested? It should seem that it had, by those who have not known what they have been meaning. Is it susceptible of any direct proof? it should seem not: for that which is used to prove every thing else, cannot itself be proved: a chain of proofs must have their commencement somewhere. To give such proof is as impossible as it is needless.

12. Not that there is or ever has been that human creature breathing, however stupid or perverse, who has not on many, perhaps on most occasions of his life, deferred to it. By the natural constitution of the human frame, on most occasions of their lives men in general embrace this principle, without thinking of it: if not for the ordering of their own actions, yet for the trying of their own actions, as well as of those of other men. There have been, at the same time, not many, perhaps, even of the most intelligent, who have been disposed to embrace it purely and without reserve. There are even few who have not taken some occasion or other to quarrel with it, either on account of their not understanding always how to apply it, or on account of some prejudice or other which they were afraid to examine into, or could not bear to part with. For such is the stuff that man is made of: in principle and in practice, in a right track and in a wrong one, the rarest of all human qualities is consistency.

Bentham says that most people, most of the time (even unconsciously) operate on the basis

of the principle of _____

_____

_____ .

13. When a man attempts to combat the principle of utility, it is with reasons drawn, without his being aware of it, from that very principle itself. His arguments, if they prove any thing, prove not that the principle is *wrong*, but that, according to the applications he supposes to be made of it, it is *misapplied*. Is it possible for a man to move the earth? Yes; but he must first find out another earth to stand upon.

Bentham's theory of utility is based on two key terms: _____

_____ and pain. Bentham is concerned with government and social reform in England. So his version of utilitarianism depends on a principle of utility that includes society. At this point in your reading, what is your own reaction to Bentham's ideas? Are his ideas good ones? Be sure to say why

you think his ideas are or are not good. _____

_____

_____

_____ .

Chapter IV: Value of a Lot of Pleasure or Pain, How to Be Measured

1. Pleasures then, and the avoidance of pains, are the *ends* which the legislator has in view: it behoves him therefore to understand their *value*. Pleasures and pains are the *instruments* he has to work with: it behoves him therefore to understand their force, which is again, in another point of view, their value.

2. To a person considered *by himself*, the value of a pleasure or pain considered *by itself*, will be greater or less, according to the four following circumstances:

1. Its *intensity*.
2. Its *duration*.
3. Its *certainty* or *uncertainty*.
4. Its *propinquity* or *remoteness*.

Use Bentham's four categories to compare two experiences. Using a scale of 1 to 10, rate eating ice cream and reading a good book. Assign a number for each of the categories and add them up. The highest score possible here would be 40.

	Eating Ice Cream	Reading a Good Book
1.	_____	_____
2.	_____	_____
3.	_____	_____
4.	_____	_____
TOTAL	_____	_____

3. These are the circumstances which are to be considered in estimating a pleasure or a pain considered each of them by itself. But when the value of any pleasure or pain is considered for the purpose of estimating the tendency of any *act* by which it is produced, there are two other circumstances to be taken into the account; these are,

> 5. Its *fecundity,* or the chance it has of being followed by sensations of the *same* kind: that is, pleasures, if it be a pleasure: pains, if it be a pain.

> 6. Its *purity,* or the chance it has of *not* being followed by sensations of the *opposite* kind: that is, pains, if it be a pleasure: pleasures, if it be a pain.

Now add Bentham's other two categories to your scores for ice cream and books. "Fecundity" means "productive," able to produce something more.

	Eating Ice Cream	Reading a Good Book
5.	_____	_____
6.	_____	_____

These two last, however, are in strictness scarcely to be deemed properties of the pleasure or the pain itself; they are not, therefore, in strictness to be taken into the account of the value of that pleasure or that pain. They are in strictness to be deemed properties only of the act, or other event, by which such pleasure or pain has been produced; and accordingly are only to be taken into the account of the tendency of such act or such event.

4. To a *number* of persons, with reference to each of whom the value of a pleasure or a pain is considered, it will be greater or less, according to seven circumstances: to wit, the six preceding ones; viz.

viz means "namely."

> 1. Its *intensity*.

> 2. Its *duration*.

3. Its *certainty* or *uncertainty*.

4. Its *propinquity* or *remoteness*.

5. Its *fecundity*.

6. Its *purity*.

And one other; to wit:

7. Its *extent*; that is, the number of persons to whom it *extends*; or (in other words) who are affected by it.

The seventh category, _____, is the category that transfers Bentham's utilitarianism into a *social* philosophy.

5. To take an exact account then of the general tendency of any act, by which the interests of a community are affected, proceed as follows. Begin with any one person of those whose interests seem most immediately to be affected by it: and take an account.

In the next few paragraphs, Bentham will describe the process of estimating the tendency for an act to be good.

1. Of the value of each distinguishable *pleasure* which appears to be produced by it in the *first* instance.

2. Of the value of each *pain* which appears to be produced by it in the *first* instance.

3. Of the value of each pleasure which appears to be produced by it *after* the first. This constitutes the *fecundity* of the first *pleasure* and the *impurity* of the first *pain*.

4. Of the value of each *pain* which appears to be produced by it after the first. This constitutes the *fecundity* of the first *pain*, and the *impurity* of the first pleasure.

5. Sum up all the values of all the *pleasures* on the one side, and those of all the *pains* on the other. The balance, if it be on the side of pleasure, will give the *good* tendency of the act upon the whole, with respect to the interests of that *individual* person; if on the side of pain, the *bad* tendency of it upon the whole.

The preceding paragraph is important. Use the space below to paraphrase or put in your own words the key ideas of this paragraph. _____

_____

_____

_____

_____ .

6. Take an account of the *number* of persons whose interests appear to be concerned; and repeat the above process with respect to each. *Sum up* the numbers expressive of the degrees of *good* tendency, which the act has, with respect to each

individual, in regard to whom the tendency of it is *good* upon the whole: do this again with respect to each individual, in regard to whom the tendency of it is *good* upon the whole; do this again with respect to each individual, in regard to whom the tendency of it is *bad* upon the whole. Take the *balance*; which, if on the side of *pleasure,* will give the general *good tendency* of the act, with respect to the total number or community of individuals concerned; if on the side of pain, the general *evil tendency,* with respect to the same community.

6. It is not to be expected that this process should be strictly pursued previously to every moral judgment, or to every legislative or judicial operation. It may, however, be always kept in view: and as near as the process actually pursued on these occasions approaches to it, so near will such process approach to the character of an exact one.

7. The same process is alike applicable to pleasure and pain, in whatever shape they appear: and by whatever denomination they are distinguished: to pleasure, whether it be called *good* (which is properly the cause or instrument of pleasure) or *profit* (which is distant pleasure, or the cause or instrument of distant pleasure,) or *convenience,* or *advantage, benefit, emolument, happiness,* and so forth: to pain, whether it be called *evil,* (which corresponds to *good*) or *mischief,* or *inconvenience,* or *disadvantage,* or *loss,* or *unhappiness,* and so forth.

8. Nor is this a novel and unwarranted, any more than it is a useless theory. In all this there is nothing but what the practice of mankind, wheresoever they have a clear view of their own interest, is perfectly conformable to. An article of property, an estate in land, for instance, is valuable, on what account? On account of the pleasures of all kinds which it enables a man to produce, and what comes to the same thing the pains of all kinds which it enables him to avert. But the value of such an article of property is universally understood to rise or fall according to the length or shortness of the time which a man has in it: the certainty or uncertainty of its coming into possession: and the nearness or remoteness of the time at which, if at all, it is to come into possession. As to the *intensity* of the pleasures which a man may derive from it, this is never thought of, because it depends upon the use which each particular person may come to make of it; which cannot be estimated till the particular pleasures he may come to derive from it, or the particular pains he may come to exclude by means of it, are brought to view. For the same reason, neither does he think of the *fecundity* or *purity* of those pleasures.

Thus much for pleasure and pain, happiness and unhappiness, in *general.* We come now to consider the several particular kinds of pain and pleasure.

One possible problem with Bentham's ideas here is that focusing on the greatest amount of good for the greatest number of people may damage, hurt, or violate the rights of a minority within a group. Can you imagine a scenario in which Bentham's argument might violate such a right? Briefly describe that scenario. ____

_____

_____

_____

_____

_____

_____

_____ .

PART 4
Readings from the Deontological or Moral Law Tradition

As was mentioned in the Introduction, the ideas in *Utilitarianism* can be seen as opposed to a long history in philosophy where the right or good thing to do is based not on the consequences of an action but on the criterion of justice or the law. This tradition is sometimes called the deontological tradition; sometimes it is referred to as the moral law tradition. (This tradition was discussed in the Introduction.) While there are many variations within this line of thought, a reading selection by Immanuel Kant will give you a classical statement of this tradition while the selection by Dr. Martin Luther King, Jr., will give you a more contemporary example.

Immanuel Kant
Foundations of the Metaphysics of Morals

Immanuel Kant's (1724–1804 C.E.) approach to ethics assumes that ethics is a rational enterprise. Reason is a prerequisite for moral decisions. Further, Kant articulates three reasons on which humans should base moral decisions. First, the reason, or "maxim," must be universal. Second, humans must not be treated as a means to an end but rather as an end in and of themselves. Third, human morality assumes autonomy; decisions are not coerced but reflect a freedom in harmony with society and nature.

In *Foundations of the Metaphysics of Morals,* Kant describes these three reasons and thus becomes a foil for Mill's views on ethics.

Kant's ideas of duty and law are connected to _____ necessity.

A priori means "before sense experience."

Since my purpose here is directed to moral philosophy, I narrow the proposed question to this: Is it not of the utmost necessity to construct a pure moral philosophy which is completely freed from everything which may be only empirical and thus belong to anthropology? That there must be such a philosophy is self-evident from the common idea of duty and moral laws. Everyone must admit that a law, if it is to hold morally, i.e., as a ground of obligation, must imply absolute necessity; he must admit that the command, "Thou shalt not lie," does not apply to men only, as if other rational beings had no need to observe it. The same is true for all other moral laws properly so called. He must concede that the ground of obligation here must not be sought in the nature of man or in the circumstances in which he is placed, but sought a priori solely in the concepts of pure reason, and that every other precept which rests on principles of mere experience, even a precept which is in certain respects universal, so far as it leans in the least on empirical grounds (perhaps only in regard to the motive involved, may be called a practical rule but never a moral law. . . .

A metaphysics of morals is therefore indispensable, not merely because of motives to speculate on the source of the a priori practical principles which lie in our reason, but also because morals themselves remain subject to all kinds of corruption so long as the guide and supreme norm for their correct estimation is lacking. For it is not sufficient to that which should be morally good that it conform to the law; it must be done for the sake of the law. Otherwise the conformity is merely contingent and spurious, because, though the unmoral ground may indeed now and then produce lawful actions, more often it brings forth unlawful ones. But the moral law can be found in its purity and genuineness (which is the central concern in the practical) nowhere else than in a pure philosophy; therefore, this (i.e., metaphysics) must lead the way, and without it there can be no moral philosophy. . . .

Nothing in the world—indeed nothing even beyond the world— can possibly be conceived which could be called good without qualification except a *good will.* Intelligence, wit, judgment, and the other talents of the mind, however they may be named, or courage, resoluteness, and perseverance as qualities of temperament, are doubtless in many respects good and desirable. But they can become extremely bad and harmful if the will, which is to make use of these gifts of nature and which in its special constitution is called character, is not good. It is the same with the gifts of fortune. . . . Thus the good will seems to constitute the indispensable condition even of worthiness to be happy. . . .

The good will is not good because of what it effects or accomplishes or because of its adequacy to achieve some proposed end; it is good only because of its willing, i.e., it is good of itself. And, regarded for itself, it is to be esteemed incomparably higher than anything which could be brought about by it in favor of any inclination or even of the sum total of all inclinations. Even if it should happen that, by a particularly unfortunate fate or by the niggardly provision of a stepmotherly nature, this will should be wholly lacking in power to accomplish its purpose, and if even the greatest effort should not avail it to achieve anything of its end, and if there remained only the good will (not as a mere wish but as the summoning of all the means in our power), it would sparkle like a jewel in its own right, as something that had its full worth in itself. Usefulness or fruitlessness can neither diminish nor augment this worth. Its usefulness would be only its setting, as it were, so as to enable us to handle it more conveniently in commerce or to attract the attention of those who are not yet connoisseurs, but

That which rests on empirical grounds is called a _____ _____ , never a moral law.

Kant is not concerned with the behavior that merely conforms to a law. Behavior must be done for the _____ the law.

Thus usually indicates that a conclusion will follow. Kant's conclusion in this paragraph is _____ _____ _____ .

Here Kant is not concerned with consequences. Rather, the good is good regardless of the ends or consequences of the action.

not to recommend it to those who are experts or to determine its worth. . . .

In the natural constitution of an organized being, i.e., one suitably adapted to life, we assume as an axiom that no organ will be found for any purpose which is not the fittest and best adapted to that purpose. Now if its preservation, its welfare—in a word, its happiness—were the real end of nature in a being having reason and will, then nature would have hit upon a very poor arrangement in appointing the reason of the creature to be the executor of this purpose. For all the actions which the creature has to perform with this intention, and the entire rule of its conduct, would be dictated much more exactly by instinct, and that end would be far more certainly attained by instinct than it ever could be by reason. And if, over and above this, reason should have been granted to the favored creature, it would have served only to let it contemplate the happy constitution of its nature, to admire it, to rejoice in it, and to be grateful for it to its beneficent cause. But reason would not have been given in order that the being should subject its faculty of desire to that weak and delusive guidance and to meddle with the purpose of nature. In a word, nature would have taken care that reason did not break forth into practical use nor have the presumption, with its weak insight, to think out for itself the plan of happiness and the means of attaining it. Nature would have taken over not only the choice of ends but also that of the means, and with wise foresight she would have entrusted both to instinct alone. . . .

Reason is not, however, competent to guide the will safely with regard to its objects and the satisfaction of all our needs (which it in part multiplies), and to this end an innate instinct would have led with far more certainty. But reason is given to us as a practical faculty, i.e., one which is meant to have an influence on the will. As nature has elsewhere distributed capacities suitable to the functions they are to perform, reason's proper function must be to produce a will good in itself and not one good merely as a means, for to the former reason is absolutely essential. This will must indeed not be the sole and complete good but the highest good and the condition of all others, even of the desire for happiness. In this case it is entirely compatible with the wisdom of nature that the cultivation of reason, which is required for the former unconditional purpose, at least in this life restricts in many ways—indeed can reduce to less than nothing—the achievement of the latter conditional purpose, happiness. For one perceives that nature here does not proceed unsuitably to its purpose, because reason, which recognizes its highest practical vocation in the establishment of a good will, is capable only of a contentment of its own kind, i.e., one that springs from the attainment of a purpose which is determined by reason, even though this injures the ends of inclination.

Underline the word *happiness* here. This is one place where Kant's ideas will be very different from J. S. Mill's.

Reason's proper function produces a will that is _____

_____,
not one that is merely a means to another end.

We have, then, to develop the concept of a will which is to be esteemed as good of itself without regard to anything else. It dwells already in the natural sound understanding and does not need so much to be taught as only to be brought to light. In the estimation of the total worth of our actions it always takes first place and is the condition of everything else. In order to show this, we shall take the concept of duty. It contains that of a good will, though with certain subjective restrictions and hindrances; but these are far from concealing it and making it unrecognizable, for they rather bring it out by contrast and make it shine forth all the brighter. . . .

Here Kant begins to describe the notion of "duty," which is not contingent on anything else.

To be kind where one can is duty, and there are, moreover, many persons so sympathetically constituted that without any motive of vanity or selfishness they find an inner satisfaction in spreading joy, and rejoice in the contentment of others which they have made possible. But I say that, however dutiful and amiable it may be, that kind of action has no true moral worth. It is on a level with [actions arising from] other inclinations, such as the inclination to honor, which, if fortunately directed to what in fact accords with duty and is generally useful and thus honorable, deserve praise and encouragement but no esteem. For the maxim lacks the moral import of an action done not from inclination but from duty. But assume that the mind of that friend to mankind was clouded by a sorrow of his own which extinguished all sympathy with the lot of others and that he still had the power to benefit others in distress, but that their need left him untouched because he was preoccupied with his own need. And now suppose him to tear himself, unsolicited by inclination, out of this dead insensibility and to perform this action only from duty and without any inclination—then for the first time his action has genuine moral worth. . . .

To secure one's own happiness is at least indirectly a duty, for discontent with one's condition under pressure from many cares and amid unsatisfied wants could easily become a great temptation to transgress duties. But without any view to duty all men have the strongest and deepest inclination to happiness, because in this idea all inclinations are summed up. But the precept of happiness is often so formulated that it definitely thwarts some inclinations, and men can make no definite and certain concept of the sum of satisfaction of all inclinations which goes under the name of happiness. It is not to be wondered at, therefore, that a single inclination, definite as to what it promises and as to the time at which it can be satisfied, can outweigh a fluctuating idea, and that, for example, a man with the gout can choose to enjoy what he likes and to suffer what he may, because according to his calculations at least on this occasion he has not sacrificed the enjoyment of the present moment to a perhaps groundless expectation of a happiness supposed to lie in health. But even in this case, if the universal inclination to happiness

For Kant, one's happiness is, at least indirectly, a _____ _____ _____.

Kant mentions "calculation" and expectation. Here he has articulated two possible problems with utilitarian thinking. Again, here is where Kant distinguishes his ideas from those of Mill.

did not determine his will, and if health were not at least for him a necessary factor in these calculations, there yet would remain, as in all other cases, a law that he ought to promote his happiness, not from inclination but from duty. Only from this law would his conduct have true moral worth. . . .

Everything in nature works according to laws. Only a rational being has the capacity of acting according to the conception of laws, i.e., according to principles. This capacity is will. Since reason is required for the derivation of actions from laws, will is nothing else than practical reason. If reason infallibly determines the will, the actions which such a being recognizes as objectively necessary are also subjectively necessary. That is, the will is a faculty of choosing only that which reason, independently of inclination, recognizes as practically necessary, i.e., as good. But if reason of itself does not sufficiently determine the will, and if the will is subjugated to subjective conditions (certain incentives) which do not always agree with objective conditions; in a word, if the will is not of itself in complete accord with reason (the actual case of men), then the actions which are recognized as objectively necessary are subjectively contingent, and the determination of such a will according to objective laws is constraint. That is, the relation of objective laws to a will which is not completely good is conceived as the determination of the will of a rational being by principles of reason to which this will is not by nature necessarily obedient.

The conception of an objective principle, so far as it constrains a will, is a command (of reason), and the formula of this command is called an *imperative*.

All imperatives are expressed by an "ought" and thereby indicate the relation of an objective law of reason to a will which is not in its subjective constitution necessarily determined by this law. This relation is that of constraint. Imperatives say that it would be good to do or to refrain from doing something, but they say it to a will which does not always do something simply because it is presented as a good thing to do. Practical good is what determines the will by means of the conception of reason and hence not by subjective causes but, rather, objectively, i.e., on grounds which are valid for every rational being as such. It is distinguished from the pleasant as that which has an influence on the will only by means of a sensation from merely subjective causes, which hold only for the senses of this or that person and not as a principle of reason which holds for everyone. . . .

All imperatives command either hypothetically or categorically. The former present the practical necessity of a possible action as a means to achieving something else which one desires (or which one may possibly desire). The categorical imperative would be one which presented an action as of itself objectively necessary, without regard to any other end.

True moral worth is not a function of happiness as an inclination, but of happiness as _____ .

Actions in accord with reason are not subjectively contingent, but _____ .

In your own words, an imperative (for Kant) is _____ .

The two categories of imperatives are (1) hypothetical; and (2) _____ .

The notion of a categorical imperative is important in understanding Kant's ideas and his thinking. Kant argues that a categorical imperative will be objectively necessary, without regard for any other end. Paraphrase or put in your own words what Kant is saying here.

For Kant, a categorical imperative is _____

_____

_____ .

Since every practical law presents a possible action as good and thus as necessary for a subject practically determinable by reason, all imperatives are formulas of the determination of action which is necessary by the principle of a will which is in any way good. If the action is good only as a means to something else, the imperative is hypothetical; but if it is thought of as good in itself, and hence as necessary in a will which of itself conforms to reason as the principle of this will, the imperative is categorical.

Underline the sentence beginning "If the action is good . . . ." Kant links reason, will, and "a good in itself" with the categorical imperative.

The imperative thus says what action possible to me would be good, and it presents the practical rule in relation to a will which does not forthwith perform an action simply because it is good, in part because the subject does not always know that the action is good and in part (when he does know it) because his maxims can still be opposed to the objective principles of practical reason.

The hypothetical imperative, therefore, says only that the action is good to some purpose, possible or actual. In the former case it is a problematical, in the latter an assertorical practical principle. The categorical imperative, which declares the action to be of itself objectively necessary without making any reference to a purpose, i.e., without having any other end, holds as an apodictical (practical) principle. . . .

There is one end, however, which we may presuppose as actual in all rational beings so far as imperatives apply to them, i.e., so far as they are dependent beings; there is one purpose not only which they *can* have but which we can presuppose that they all *do* have by a necessity of nature. This purpose is happiness. The hypothetical imperative which represents the practical necessity of action as means to the promotion of happiness is an assertorical imperative. We may not expound it as merely necessary to an uncertain and a merely possible purpose, but as necessary to a purpose which we can a priori and with assurance assume for everyone because it belongs to his essence. Skill in the choice of means to one's own highest welfare can be called prudence in the narrowest sense. Thus the imperative which refers to the choice of means to one's own happiness, i.e., the precept of prudence, is still only

A hypothetical imperative is merely a means to _____ .

hypothetical; the action is not absolutely commanded but commanded only as a means to another end.

Finally, there is one imperative which directly commands a certain conduct without making its condition some purpose to be reached by it. This imperative is categorical. It concerns not the material of the action and its intended result but the form and the principle from which it results. What is essentially good in it consists in the intention, the result being what it may. This imperative may be called the imperative of morality. . . .

If I think of a hypothetical imperative as such, I do not know what it will contain until the condition is stated [under which it is an imperative]. But if I think of a categorical imperative, I know immediately what it contains. For since the imperative contains besides the law only the necessity that the maxim should accord with this law, while the law contains no condition to which it is restricted, there is nothing remaining in it except the universality of law as such to which the maxim of the action should conform; and in effect this conformity alone is represented as necessary by the imperative.

Underline this paragraph. It is one of the most famous sections in philosophy. Kant's categorical imperative will be a reference point for much of ethical theory in the nineteenth and twentieth centuries.

There is, therefore, only one categorical imperative. It is: Act only according to that maxim by which you can at the same time will that it should become a universal law.

Now if all imperatives of duty can be derived from this one imperative as a principle, we can at least show what we understand by the concept of duty and what it means, even though it remain undecided whether that which is called duty is an empty concept or not.

Is this phrasing different from the previous statement of the categorical imperative?

The universality of law according to which effects are produced constitutes what is properly called nature in the most general sense (as to form), i.e., the existence of things so far as it is determined by universal laws. [By analogy], then, the universal imperative of duty can be expressed as follows: Act as though the maxim of your action were by your will to become a universal law of nature. . . .

The categorical imperative is important both in Kant's ideas and in the history of ethics. In your own words, restate Kant's categorical imperative. *The categorical imperative is:* _____

_____

_____

_____

_____ .

Now, I say, man and, in general, every rational being exists as an end in himself and not merely as a means to be arbitrarily used by this or that will. In all his actions, whether they are directed to himself or to other rational beings, he must always be regarded at the same time as an end. All objects of inclinations have only a conditional worth, for if the inclinations and the needs founded on them did not exist, their object would be without worth. The inclinations themselves as the sources of needs, however, are so lacking in absolute worth that the universal wish of every rational being must be indeed to free himself completely from them. Therefore, the worth of any objects to be obtained by our actions is at all times conditional. Beings whose existence does not depend on our will but on nature, if they are not rational beings, have only a relative worth as means and are therefore called "things"; on the other hand, rational beings are designated "persons" because their nature indicates that they are ends in themselves, i.e., things which may not be used merely as means. Such a being is thus an object of respect and, so far, restricts all [arbitrary] choice. Such beings are not merely subjective ends whose existence as a result of our action has a worth for us, but are objective ends, i.e., beings whose existence in itself is an end. Such an end is one for which no other end can be substituted, to which these beings should serve merely as means. For, without them, nothing of absolute worth could be found, and if all worth is conditional and thus contingent, no supreme practical principle for reason could be found anywhere.

Thus if there is to be a supreme practical principle and a categorical imperative for the human will, it must be one that forms an objective principle of the will from the conception of that which is necessarily an end for everyone because it is an end in itself. Hence this objective principle can serve as a universal practical law. The ground of this principle is: rational nature exists as an end in itself. Man necessarily thinks of his own existence in this way; thus far it is a subjective principle of human actions. Also every other rational being thinks of his existence by means of the same rational ground which holds also for myself; thus it is at the same time an objective principle from which, as a supreme practical ground, it must be possible to derive all laws of the will. The practical imperative, therefore, is the following: Act so that you treat humanity, whether in your own person or in that of another, always as an end and never as a means only. Let us now see whether this can be achieved.

Underline the sentence beginning "Now, I say man . . . ." This is another famous passage from Kant's philosophy.

A person should always be treated as an _____ and never as a _____.

Imagine a scenario in which a person is being treated by another person as a means to an end rather than as an end in and of him- or herself. Describe that scenario. _____

_____

_____

_____

_____.

Is such a situation always wrong? What would Kant say? ____

_____ What would you say? _____

_____

_____.

Martin Luther King, Jr.
Letter from Birmingham Jail

In 1963, in the midst of the "early civil rights movement" in America, Dr. Martin Luther King, Jr., and the Southern Christian Leadership Council participated in an economic boycott of white-owned stores in Birmingham, Alabama. Reflecting the religious division of the time, eight white religious leaders in Alabama called the boycott inappropriate at that time. King's response is his "Letter from Birmingham Jail." In this selection, justice or moral law transcends evil civil laws just as it transcends any utilitarian considerations that possible violence will result from nonviolent actions like the boycott or that disorder and chaos must be avoided for the good of the majority of the people. "An unjust law is no law at all" and "peace is not peace without justice" describe King's ideas. In language that is often poetic, prophetic, and, at the same time, clearly reasoned, King provides a counterpoint to Mill's ethical point in *Utilitarianism*.

April 16, 1963

My Dear Fellow Clergymen:

While confined here in the Birmingham city jail, I came across your recent statement calling my present activities "unwise and untimely." Seldom do I pause to answer criticism of my work and ideas. If I sought to answer all the criticisms that cross my desk, my secretaries would have little time for anything other than such correspondence in the course of the day, and I would have no time for constructive work. But since I feel that you are men of genuine good will and that your criticisms are sincerely set forth, I want to try to answer your statement in what I hope will be patient and reasonable terms.

I think I should indicate why I am here in Birmingham, since you have been influenced by the view which argues against "outsiders coming in." I have the honor of serving as president of the Southern Christian Leadership Conference, an organization operating in every southern state, with headquarters in Atlanta, Georgia. We have some eighty-five affiliated organizations across the South, and one of them is the Alabama Christian Movement for Human Rights. Frequently we share staff, educational and financial resources with our affiliates. Several months ago the affiliate here in Birmingham asked us to be on call to engage in a nonviolent direct-action program if such were deemed necessary. We readily consented, and when the hour came we lived up to our promise. So I, along with several members of my staff, am here because I was invited here. I am here because I have organizational ties here.

But more basically, I am in Birmingham because injustice is here. Just as the prophets of the eighth century B.C. left their villages and carried their "thus saith the Lord" far beyond the boundaries of their home towns, and just as the Apostle Paul left his village of Tarsus and carried the gospel of Jesus Christ to the far corners of the Greco-Roman world, so am I compelled to carry the gospel of freedom beyond my own home town. Like Paul, I must constantly respond to the Macedonian call for aid.

Moreover, I am cognizant of the interrelatedness of all communities and states. I cannot sit idly by in Atlanta and not be concerned about what happens in Birmingham. Injustice anywhere is a threat to justice everywhere. We are caught in an inescapable network of mutuality, tied in a single garment of destiny. Whatever affects one directly, affects all indirectly. Never again can we afford to live with the narrow, provincial "outside agitator" idea. Anyone who lives inside the United States can never be considered an outsider anywhere within its bounds.

You deplore the demonstrations taking place in Birmingham. But your statement, I am sorry to say, fails to express a similar concern for the conditions that brought about the demonstrations. I am sure that none of you would want to rest content with the superficial kind of social analysis that deals merely with effects and does not grapple with underlying causes. It is unfortunate that demonstrations are taking place in Birmingham, but it is even more unfortunate that the city's white power structure left the Negro community with no alternative.

In any nonviolent campaign there are four basic steps: collection of the facts to determine whether injustices exist; negotiation;

King is in Birmingham because

_____ .

The images and references in this paragraph are to the biblical tradition.

In this paragraph, King is

concerned with the _____ of all communities and states.

self-purification; and direct action. We have gone through all these steps in Birmingham. . . .

We know through painful experience that freedom is never voluntarily given by the oppressor; it must be demanded by the oppressed. Frankly, I have yet to engage in a direct-action campaign that was "well timed" in the view of those who have not suffered unduly from the disease of segregation. For years now I have heard the word "Wait!" It rings in the ear of every Negro with piercing familiarity. This "Wait" has almost always meant "Never." We must come to see, with one of our distinguished jurists, that "justice too long delayed is justice denied."

We have waited for more than 340 years for our constitutional and God-given rights. The nations of Asia and Africa are moving with jetlike speed toward gaining political independence, but we still creep at horse-and-buggy pace toward gaining a cup of coffee at a lunch counter. Perhaps it is easy for those who have never felt the stinging darts of segregation to say, "Wait." But when you have seen vicious mobs lynch your mothers and fathers at will and drown your sisters and brothers at whim; when you have seen hate-filled policemen curse, kick and even kill your black brothers and sisters; when you see the vast majority of your twenty million Negro brothers smothering in an airtight cage of poverty in the midst of an affluent society; when you suddenly find your tongue twisted and your speech stammering as you seek to explain to your six-year-old daughter why she can't go to the public amusement park that has just been advertised on television, and see tears welling up in her eyes when she is told that Funtown is closed to colored children, and see ominous clouds of inferiority beginning to form in her little mental sky, and see her beginning to distort her personality by developing an unconscious bitterness toward white people; when you have to concoct an answer for a five-year-old son who is asking: "Daddy, why do white people treat colored people so mean?"; when you take a cross-country drive and find it necessary to sleep night after night in the uncomfortable corners of your automobile because no motel will accept you; when you are humiliated day in and day out by nagging signs reading "white" and "colored"; when your first name becomes "nigger," your middle name becomes "boy" (however old you are) and your last name becomes "John," and your wife and mother are never given the respected title "Mrs."; when you are harried by day and haunted by night by the fact that you are a Negro, living constantly at tiptoe stance, never quite knowing what to expect next, and are plagued with inner fears and outer resentments; when you are forever fighting a degenerating sense of "nobodiness"—then you will understand why we find it difficult to wait. There comes a time when the cup of endurance runs over, and men are no longer willing to be plunged into the abyss of

The reference is to *Brown v. Board of Education*.

For King, there are two types of laws, _____ laws and _____ laws.

Augustine was an important early Christian theologian and philosopher. He lived in the fourth and fifth centuries C.E. and served as a bishop of the church in North Africa.

Aquinas was a thirteenth-century Christian theologian.

A law is just if it _____ . A law is unjust if it _____ .

Martin Buber was a twentieth-century Jewish theologian and philosopher.

Paul Tillich was a twentieth-century Christian theologian and philosopher.

despair. I hope, sirs, you can understand our legitimate and unavoidable impatience.

You express a great deal of anxiety over our willingness to break laws. This is certainly a legitimate concern. Since we so diligently urge people to obey the Supreme Court's decision of 1954 outlawing segregation in the public schools, at first glance it may seem rather paradoxical for us consciously to break laws. One may well ask: "How can you advocate breaking some laws and obeying others?" The answer lies in the fact that there are two types of laws: just and unjust. I would be the first to advocate obeying just laws. One has not only a legal but a moral responsibility to obey just laws. Conversely, one has a moral responsibility to disobey unjust laws. I would agree with St. Augustine that "an unjust law is no law at all."

Now, what is the difference between the two? How does one determine whether a law is just or unjust? A just law is a man-made code that squares with the moral law or the law of God. An unjust law is a code that is out of harmony with the moral law. To put it in the terms of St. Thomas Aquinas: An unjust law is a human law that is not rooted in eternal law and natural law. Any law that uplifts human personality is just. Any law that degrades human personality is unjust. All segregation statutes are unjust because segregation distorts the soul and damages the personality. It gives the segregator a false sense of superiority and the segregated a false sense of inferiority. Segregation, to use the terminology of the Jewish philosopher Martin Buber, substitutes an "I–it" relationship for an "I–thou" relationship and ends up relegating persons to the status of things. Hence segregation is not only politically, economically and sociologically unsound, it is morally wrong and sinful. Paul Tillich has said that sin is separation. Is not segregation an existential expression of man's tragic separation, his awful estrangement, his terrible sinfulness? Thus it is that I can urge men to obey the 1954 decision of the Supreme Court, for it is morally right; and I can urge them to disobey segregation ordinances, for they are morally wrong. . . .

Sometimes a law is just on its face and unjust in its application. For instance, I have been arrested on a charge of parading without a permit. Now, there is nothing wrong in having an ordinance which requires a permit for a parade. But such an ordinance becomes unjust when it is used to maintain segregation and to deny citizens the First-Amendment privilege of peaceful assembly and protest.

I hope you are able to see the distinction I am trying to point out. In no sense do I advocate evading or defying the law, as would the rabid segregationist. That would lead to anarchy. One who breaks an unjust law must do so openly, lovingly, and with a willingness to accept the penalty. I submit that an individual who breaks a law that conscience tells him is unjust, and who willingly accepts the penalty of imprisonment in order to arouse the conscience of the community over its injustice, is in reality expressing the highest respect for law.

Of course, there is nothing new about this kind of civil disobedience. It was evidenced sublimely in the refusal of Shadrach, Meshach and Abednego to obey the laws of Nebuchadnezzar, on the ground that a higher moral law was at stake. It was practiced superbly by the early Christians, who were willing to face hungry lions and the excruciating pain of chopping blocks rather than submit to certain unjust laws of the Roman Empire. To a degree, academic freedom is a reality today because Socrates practiced civil disobedience. In our own nation, the Boston Tea Party represented a massive act of civil disobedience.

We should never forget that everything Adolf Hitler did in Germany was ''legal'' and everything the Hungarian freedom fighters did in Hungary was ''illegal.'' It was ''illegal'' to aid and comfort a Jew in Hitler's Germany. Even so, I am sure that, had I lived in Germany at the time, I would have aided and comforted my Jewish brothers. If today I lived in a Communist country where certain principles dear to a Christian faith are suppressed, I would openly advocate disobeying that country's antireligious laws . . . .

In your statement you assert that our actions, even though peaceful, must be condemned because they precipitate violence. But is this a logical assertion? Isn't this like condemning a robbed man because his possession of money precipitated the evil act of robbery? Isn't this like condemning Socrates because his unswerving commitment to truth and his philosophical inquiries precipitated the act by the misguided populace in which they made him drink hemlock? Isn't this like condemning Jesus because his unique God-consciousness and never-ceasing devotion to God's will precipitated the evil act of crucifixion? We must come to see that, as the federal courts have consistently affirmed, it is wrong to urge an individual to cease his efforts to gain his basic constitutional rights because the quest may precipitate violence. Society must protect the robbed and punish the robber . . . .

Before closing I feel impelled to mention one other point in your statement that has troubled me profoundly. You warmly commended the Birmingham police force for keeping ''order'' and ''preventing violence.'' I doubt that you would have so warmly commended the police force if you had seen its dogs sinking their teeth into unarmed, nonviolent Negroes. I doubt that you would so quickly commend the policemen if you were to observe their ugly and inhumane treatment of Negroes here in the city jail; if you were to watch them push and curse old Negro women and young Negro girls; if you were to see them slap and kick old Negro men and young

If someone openly breaks an unjust law, King argues that this person is expressing high _____ for the law.

This reference is to the story in the biblical Book of Daniel.

Socrates was a Greek philosopher who died in 399 B.C.E. He was the teacher of Plato.

Read this section slowly. Note the force of the language and the rhetoric.

boys; if you were to observe them, as they did on two occasions, refuse to give us food because we wanted to sing our grace together. I cannot join you in your praise of the Birmingham police department.

It is true that the police have exercised a degree of discipline in handling the demonstrators. In this sense they have conducted themselves rather "nonviolently" in public. But for what purpose? To preserve the evil system of segregation. Over the past few years I have consistently preached that nonviolence demands that the means we use must be as pure as the ends we seek. I have tried to make clear that it is wrong to use immoral means to attain moral ends. But now I must affirm that it is just as wrong, or perhaps even more so, to use moral means to preserve immoral ends. Perhaps Mr. Connor and his policemen have been rather nonviolent in public, as was Chief Pritchett in Albany, Georgia, but they have used the moral means of nonviolence to maintain the immoral end of racial injustice. As. T. S. Eliot has said: "The last temptation is the greatest treason: To do the right deed for the wrong reason."

I wish you had commended the Negro sit-inners and demonstrators of Birmingham for their sublime courage, their willingness to suffer and their amazing discipline in the midst of great provocation. One day the South will recognize its real heroes. They will be the James Merediths, with the noble sense of purpose that enables them to face jeering and hostile mobs, and with the agonizing loneliness that characterizes the life of the pioneer. They will be old, oppressed, battered Negro women, symbolized in a seventy-two-year-old woman in Montgomery, Alabama, who rose up with a sense of dignity and with her people decided not to ride segregated buses, and who responded with ungrammatical profundity to one who inquired about her weariness: "My feets is tired, but my soul is at rest." They will be the young high school and college students, the young ministers of the gospel and a host of their elders, courageously and nonviolently sitting in at lunch counters and willingly going to jail for conscience' sake. One day the South will know that when these disinherited children of God sat down at lunch counters, they were in reality standing up for what is best in the American dream and for the most sacred values in our Judaeo-Christian heritage, thereby bringing our nation back to those great wells of democracy which were dug deep by the founding fathers in their formulation of the Constitution and the Declaration of Independence.

Never before have I written so long a letter. I'm afraid it is much too long to take your precious time. I can assure you that it would have been much shorter if I had been writing from a comfortable desk, but what else can one do when he is alone in a narrow cell, other than write long letters, think long thoughts and pray long prayers?

If I have said anything in this letter that overstates the truth and indicates an unreasonable impatience, I beg you to forgive me. If I have said anything that understates the truth and indicates my having a patience that allows me to settle for anything less than brotherhood, I beg God to forgive me.

I hope this letter finds you strong in the faith. I also hope that circumstances will soon make it possible for me to meet each of you, not as an integrationist or a civil-rights leader but as a fellow clergyman and a Christian brother. Let us all hope that the dark clouds of racial prejudice will soon pass away and the deep fog of misunderstanding will be lifted from our fear-drenched communities, and in some not too distant tomorrow the radiant stars of love and brotherhood will shine over our great nation with all their scintillating beauty.

Yours for the cause of Peace and Brotherhood,
MARTIN LUTHER KING, JR.

King's argument is based on the distinction between just and unjust laws. Do you think that there are (or have been) laws that

were unjust? _____. If you said "no," can you imagine a

place or a time when there could be unjust laws? _____.
What is your reaction to King's language in this selection?

_____

Do you think a Buddhist, a Hindu, or an atheist would be able

to agree with King's ideas? _____ Why or why not?

_____

_____

_____

Appendix
Writing About Ethics and John Stuart Mill

This portion of the tour gives you an opportunity to think and reflect—within the process of writing—about the issues of ethics that have been raised in *Utilitarianism* and in the traditions of utilitarianism and deontology. The writing exercises also nurture certain "intellectual virtues"—habits of thought or attitudes of the mind that transcend the discipline of philosophy or ethics. While the notion of intellectual virtues is used in a variety of contexts in literature on critical thinking and in theories of higher education, I take it to refer to at least three components: simple location, complex location, and appreciation of judgment.[1] In more familiar terms, "simple location" refers to the ability to describe something, without destructive biases or distortion. In spite of the adjective *simple*, this process of locating or describing is often difficult. Secondly, "complex location" refers to the ability to bring into relationship more than one description. In the university this often takes the form of "compare and contrast" exercises. While valuable, this ability or intellectual virtue depends on the previous virtue—description or location. Finally, "appreciation of judgment" refers to the ability to apply ideas, theories, descriptions, terms, and frameworks to a particular situation. Each of these intellectual virtues are related, but the following writing tasks are intended to proceed from the simplest to the most complex.

---

[1] James H. Foard, "Writing Across the Curriculum: A Religious Studies Contribution," in *Beyond the Classics? Essays in Religious Studies and Liberal Education,* eds. Frank E. Reynolds and Sheryl Burkhalter (Atlanta: Scholars Press, 1990), pp. 203–217.

If the guided tour format assists in slowing down your reading of classic texts in philosophy, this section of the tour is intended to slow down the writing process and, consequently, the processes of thinking and reflection.

Description: Writing for "Simple Location"

Often you will be asked to describe, explain, or "locate" something and make sure that your description, or communication, has crossed over to your audience. Whether you are describing a new product or a new process to a supervisor, training a new coworker, explaining to your son or daughter how electricity works, or telling fellow students about a certain class they are about to take, you are practicing the intellectual virtue of "simple location"—the ability to describe something. This intellectual virtue includes the basis for most communication—the ability to translate your experience or your "location" to another. Here is the writing task that will give you a chance to practice the intellectual virtue that we call "simple location."

Imagine that you are writing to a student in a senior English class at a Japanese women's university in Hiroshima, Japan. Since these women are seniors, ordinary English language is not a problem. However, none of these women is a philosophy major and none of them have taken classes in Western philosophy during their stay at the university. Your task is to write a short, three-page letter in which you briefly introduce yourself to your audience; describe Mill's key ideas of ethics, giving examples and illustrations where necessary; and describe why Mill's ideas are remembered in Western philosophy.

Here is an outline format for the task:

    I. Personal introduction (1/2–3/4 page)
   II. Description of Mill's ideas (1–1/2 pages)
      A. Ideas
      B. Examples
  III. Description of the importance of Mill's ideas to Western philosophy (1 page)

When you finish writing you will have practiced the intellectual virtue of "simple location." The choice of audience here is deliberate. As your audience changes, the way you "locate," or describe, your own experience of an idea or event also changes. The way you describe a New Year's Eve party to a parent is probably not the same way you would describe that party to your best friend. For this writing task, of course, you do not know much about the community or the people you are addressing. You will be "inventing" or imagining your audience. Most of the time in the university, you will be doing this unconsciously if not consciously. You know a bit about your instructor. But as you are writing your paper for her or him, you are, in fact, inventing your audience. As I am writing this text, I am inventing or imagining my audience—you. This writing task is not designed to have you do research into another culture. It is designed to have you reflect on the way the audience functions in your writing and changes the process of location or description.

Bringing Into Relation: Writing For "Complex Location"

The second intellectual virtue requires not only that you be skilled in simple location or description, but also that you be able to bring your "locations" into relation with each other.

Imagine that you are writing a four-page letter to Martin Luther King, Jr. Your task is briefly to introduce yourself; to articulate your understanding of his ideas that you recently read in his "Letter from Birmingham Jail"; to articulate Mill's ideas about ethics, and finally (this is the "complex location") to distill the one idea or image or point or assertion that differentiates Mill's ideas from King's ideas. Be sure to explain why that one point is crucial.

Here is an outline format for the task:

 I. Personal introduction (1/2–3/4 page)
 II. Your understanding of King's ideas (1 page)
 III. Your understanding of Mill's ideas (1 page)
 IV. Your understanding of the differences between King and Mill (1–1-1/2 pages)

To understand something, it is often necessary to bring in "difference"—a different opinion, idea, or perspective. The contrast clarifies your understanding of the original idea. In this sense, people often need "the other" to understand themselves. When you have finished this writing task, you will have had to (1) empathetically understand at least two divergent views and (2) notice the difference. You will have practiced "complex location."

Application: Writing for "Appreciation of Judgment"

The third intellectual virtue in this section of the tour is "appreciation of judgment," or application. This intellectual virtue assumes the previous intellectual virtues of "simple location" and "complex location." But the ability to apply ideas and theories to contemporary situations is based on the ability to describe clearly, note similarities and differences, and (this is the most complex part), apply the ideas to something in life. To do this you must make judgments, and you must appreciate the difficulty inherent within the process, as well as the need to justify, explain, or give reasons for a particular judgment.

A medical doctor from Michigan has recently been in the news for assisting some of his patients in bringing about their own deaths. (This is somewhat awkwardly phrased because language often betrays a particular perspective. I have tried to remain as neutral as possible in describing this situation. ''Simple location'' is not so simple!) This doctor has built a device and provided the opportunity for patients to inject themselves with a drug that will end their lives. Your task is to write this doctor a letter. In the letter, briefly introduce yourself to Dr. M. (for Michigan). Then state clearly whether you think what he is doing is right. (Hint: Do not worry about the legal matters; focus on ethics.) Finally, clearly give the reasons for your judgment. This task asks you to apply the ideas learned in your reading and in your class, to make a judgment, and to give reasons for that judgment. Be sure to mention the ideas and concepts you have encountered in our tour or in your class.

Here is an outline format for the task:

   I. Personal introduction (1/2–3/4 pages)
  II. Your judgment (1 page)
 III. Your reasons for your judgment (2–3 pages)

When you have completed these three writing tasks, you will have practiced, through writing, three intellectual virtues—habits of thought or attitudes of mind which the editor of this book values. The editor chose the letter format for the assignments to help guarantee that your responses would be personal and to focus the energy needed to ''invent the audience.'' Furthermore, the editor designed the assignments to prevent you from adopting, without reflection, the genre of the ''university essay.''

Suggested Reading

Works by John Stuart Mill

1843—*A System of Logic*

1844—*Essays on Some Unsettled Questions of Political Economy*

1848—*The Principles of Political Economy*

1859-75—*Dissertations and Discussions* (an anthology of Mill's periodical writings, 2 volumes in 1859, one in 1867, and one in 1875)

1859—*On Liberty*

1859—*Thoughts on Parliamentary Reform*

1861—*Considerations on Representative Government*

1863—*Utilitarianism* (reprint from *Fraser's Magazine,* 1861)

1865—*An Examination of Sir William Hamilton's Philosophy*

1865—*August Comte and Positivism*

1869—*The Subjection of Women*

1873—*Autobiography* (published posthumously)

1874—*Three Essays on Religion* (published posthumously)

1879—*Chapters on Socialism* (published posthumously)

The Collected Works of John Stuart Mill are published by the University of Toronto Press, Toronto, Canada.

Secondary Sources

Carlisle, Janice. *John Stuart Mill and the Writing of Character.* Athens: University of Georgia Press, 1991. In this recent work, the author argues that character was the principle subject of Mill's career as a writer and the central fact of his experience. Mill's work thus focuses around ethology, the science of the formation of character by particular circumstances.

Glassman, Peter. *J. S. Mill: The Evolution of a Genius.* Gainesville: University of Florida Press, 1985. Admittedly using an "impressionistic and speculative method," this author applies the categories of literary criticism and psychoanalysis to the life and work of Mill. Thus his book becomes a history of Mill's literary and psychological creation.

Alan Ryan. *J. S. Mill.* Boston: Routledge & Kegan Paul, 1974. This book is from a series designed to offer for "nonspecialist readers," students, and the general public, "clear and systematic accounts of the life and times and works" of a variety of authors.

Alan Ryan. *John Stuart Mill.* 2d ed. Atlantic Heights, NJ: Humanities Press International, 1990. The first edition of this book (1970) was admittedly a piece of "propaganda" attempting to show that Mill was a systematic thinker and that *A System of Logic* was the key to the unity of his thought. The preface to the second edition acknowledges the changes and the development of Mill scholarship since 1970.

Benard Semmel. *John Stuart Mill and the Pursuit of Virtue.* New Haven: Yale University Press, 1984. This author takes a less technical approach, which places Mill in the broad history of ideas. The work interlocks ethics, philosophy, and history.

John Skorupski. *John Stuart Mill.* New York: Routledge, 1989. This book is from a series focusing on the arguments of philosophers. This is a comprehensive survey of Mill's ideas from language to logic to ethics. But there is an emphasis on four works: *A System of Logic, Examination of Sir William Hamilton's Philosophy, Utilitarianism,* and *On Liberty.*